Rural Education
in America

Rural Education in America

What Works for Our Students, Teachers, and Communities

GEOFF MARIETTA AND SKY MARIETTA

HARVARD EDUCATION PRESS
Cambridge, Massachusetts

Paperback ISBN 978-1-68253-560-8
Library Edition ISBN 978-1-68253-561-5
Library of Congress Cataloging-in-Publication Data is on file.

Published by Harvard Education Press,
an imprint of the Harvard Education Publishing Group

Harvard Education Press
8 Story Street
Cambridge, MA 02138

Cover Design: Ciano Design
Cover Image: Pierre Leclerc Photography/Moment via Getty Images.

The typefaces used in this book are Joanna Nova, Joanna Sans Nova, and Archer.

To our own children,
Harlan and Perry,
and to all schoolchildren
growing up and learning
in rural America.

CONTENTS

Introduction   1

PART I
The Rural Context

1 From the Outside Looking In: Rural Education Today   17

2 From the Inside Looking In: The Strengths of Rural
  Communities   37

3 The Forces Shaping Rural Education   53

PART II
Meeting the Needs of Rural Students

4 Early Childhood Education and Care   71

5 Literacy for Rural Children   89

6 STEM Education in Rural Communities   111

7 College and Career Readiness   129

PART III

Moving to Action

8 Putting It Together: A Plan for Rural Schools   147

9 Promises and Pitfalls of Serving Rural Education   169

   Notes   187

   About the Authors   217

   Index   219

INTRODUCTION

THE SCHOOL SITS on top of a hill in a small neighborhood of modest homes, surrounded in every direction by the ancient slopes of the Appalachian Mountains. There is one particularly formidable ridge visible to the south, and it is the same mountain that once blocked westward expansion so completely that it took Daniel Boone on a journey twenty miles to the east to find passage at the Cumberland Gap. The concrete block walls of the school and bright vinyl wraps over the windows speak to a new era, although many would consider a preK–12 school like this one as belonging to an old-fashioned era of education. Inside this building are around eight hundred students of all ages, including preschoolers as young as three walking along the same hallways as teenagers enrolled in high school.

This is Williamsburg Independent School, a Title I preK–12 school in Appalachian Kentucky. The school serves an economically distressed community, and currently more than 70 percent of its students qualify for free or reduced-price lunch. We have spent quite a bit of time in this building, getting to know the students and teachers through cake walks and basketball games. We see the crossing guards in the morning and know that the superintendent greets the preschool students by name as they arrive every day. When the bell rings at three p.m., we see the mixed-age throng of children streaming out, some to cars and buses and others to walk home. But the reasons for this deep familiarity may surprise some. No, we are not researchers who have studied this school, nor are we teachers or educational consultants brought in to lead a strategic improvement process. Instead, we, the authors, are the parents of two boys who go here each day for school. At the time of this writing our older child is in fourth grade and the younger is finishing up his second year of preschool, already gunning for kindergarten in the fall.

If you are wondering why we live in a rural and poor part of the Kentucky mountains, we can assure you it is for the most ordinary of reasons. But first, let's back up and do an introduction. We are Geoff and Sky, and both of us have spent our professional lives thinking about the well-being of rural children and communities. Geoff was born in Hibbing on the Mesabi Iron Range in northern Minnesota. He attended the University of Montana, where a job working overnights at a children's shelter set him on a trajectory to becoming a special education teacher. Sky grew up in Berea, Kentucky, the fifth of seven children in a household that subsisted at less than half the poverty level her entire childhood. She went from public school to Yale University, where she was shocked to learn about the expected outcomes for children like herself. She knew that education had changed her life, so she wanted to be an elementary teacher.

And this is where our lives connected. We both joined Teach for America, sought out a rural placement, and found ourselves working for the Gallup-McKinley County School District on the Navajo Nation in New Mexico. Although we worked for the same district, we lived seventy miles apart. We first met at the Rough Rock Rodeo, where Sky made fun of Geoff for wearing overalls and Geoff thought Sky was a stuck-up snob from Yale. But over time, and over many, many hours spent compiling our professional teaching portfolios together, those initial bad feelings wore off. When we began dating, Sky was working at the smallest and most remote school in the district, and when it closed due to low enrollment she moved to the town of Gallup. Geoff started off as a high school special education teacher, focused on helping students with emotional and behavioral disturbances, and then was promoted to assistant principal. Shortly after Sky settled at her new school, he was promoted again to a district position helping lead particularly difficult IEP (Individualized Education Program) meetings in a school district that is larger in land size than the state of Delaware.

It did not take long working as teachers and instructional leaders to get frustrated with the resources available to help our students. Poverty is a pernicious issue that our country has been wrestling with for generations, and some rural areas like Native nations and Appalachia have been in and out of the national spotlight for their dire struggles for generations. Although there may be a collective awareness of challenges in rural America, we found that nearly all educational resources for children living in poverty were focused on urban schools. Indeed, "urban school" had almost become synonymous with "poor school." The specific students we worked with—rural Indigenous students who either had a disability or were learning English as a second language—were particularly absent from the textbooks and articles on education we read as we pursued our master's degrees. But neither did we see our own home communities—rural towns that followed the booms and busts of the resource extraction industry—represented in the best practices and ideas that were handed out as solutions to educators like ourselves.

And so we went off to graduate school, determined to advance our knowledge and add a rural perspective. Geoff, who had been focused on school leadership, was accepted at Harvard Business

School (HBS). A few months later Sky was accepted to the Harvard Graduate School of Education (HGSE). But first we stopped along the way to get married at Pine Mountain Settlement School, a remote and scenic school campus turned nonprofit in the heart of Appalachian coal country, where Sky's mother had been an elementary teacher. At HBS, Geoff found himself drawn to the initiatives that focused on education, and after graduating ended up joining HGSE for his doctorate. Sky focused on early language and literacy development and began her dissertation research in her native Appalachia. In all, we spent eleven years in Cambridge, and although we did continue to work in Eastern Kentucky, we were mostly immersed in the issues facing urban schools. Geoff led urban district teams through strategic planning processes, as well as worked on ways unions and districts could work together better.[1] And Sky too spent most of her time with urban school leaders, focusing on language and literacy skills, particularly for English language learners.[2]

This is how we found ourselves on a path toward careers as academics, studying primarily urban problems and urban-focused strategies. But this is where the story also shifts. Geoff was getting ready to graduate from his program and was entering the job market. Sky, who had been working as a postdoctoral fellow and lecturer at HGSE, was pregnant with their second child and looking for jobs as the trailing spouse. But at the same time Sky's mother, back home in Kentucky, was dying of bone marrow cancer. When the position of executive director of Pine Mountain Settlement School came open, it was a wild-card option, but it also represented an opportunity to go back home and spend precious remaining time with Sky's mom. The two of us looked at the organization and decided it needed Geoff's skills the most. He put in an application, and our advisors and family were surprised when we decided that this small educational nonprofit would be our next step, turning away university positions to immerse ourselves in the day-to-day needs of rural Appalachia.[3]

Exactly one month before Donald Trump announced his candidacy for president in 2015, we loaded up a sixteen-foot U-Haul and moved from Harvard Square in Cambridge, Massachusetts, to Pine Mountain Settlement School in Harlan County, Kentucky. The campus sits on the north side of Pine Mountain, a 125-mile-long mountain that is crossed by roads in only seven places in its entire stretch. This was the very heart of Appalachian coal country, a place of high mountain walls and narrow valleys where you have to be careful if you leave trash out or you will attract bears. It is also a place where the opioid epidemic, chronic poverty, and poor health outcomes have devastated communities for decades. Still, we found a lot to love about our new home. It is situated in one of the most biodiverse places in the Northern Hemisphere, a temperate rainforest where there are hundreds of species of blooming plants, and where mountains form in endless waves of blues and greens. Not only was there incredible natural beauty, but we also found tight-knit communities where folks hunted for meat, planted their own vegetables, and cared very deeply about those around them. When Sky's mother died less than a month after we moved, we were overwhelmed by how our grief was softened by a communal ownership of the loss, including people who wept openly with us.

In a different political era, our return to our roots under these conditions would probably not receive much attention. Instead, as the 2016 presidential election unfolded, a new dialogue emerged about rural America, and the coalfields of Appalachia in particular. Suddenly, this part of America that had sacrificed tremendously to provide coal-fired energy to our country became an easy target for ridicule and contempt. These narratives about rural America confused us and conflicted with what we knew and had experienced, both in our childhoods and in our current experience as professionals and parents raising our children in the region. But this national dialogue on urban-rural divides also seemed unimportant given the problems we were trying to solve every day. All around us were families who were desperate for work, who loved their children and wanted the best for them, but were trying to overcome the terrible circumstances that arise under the great pressure of poverty.

For community members who did not have access to clean water, the spigot at our campus was the place they filled up their containers. When we saw a young mother out walking as a prostitute, we gave her a chance to get clean and set her life on track. When a staff member faced certain harm at home, the campus became her shelter. We did not see voters or political parties; instead, we saw people and families and children. And those people were smart, resilient, and far more diverse than what we saw represented in the public narrative.

We believe that rural America has been greatly misunderstood. Not only by news media and pundits, but also by policy makers and politicians, and even, at times, the scholars who turn their eye on rural people. Appalachia is only the very tip of an iceberg of misperception and confusion. Collectively, rural America represents a dizzying array of people and circumstances. In fact, the very diversity of rural America may be its core feature. Not only does that diversity emerge in race and social class, in rural towns both rich and poor, but in the very complexity of the rural experience.

We certainly bring our own lens as community members and practitioners, but living in rural America is a constant reminder that the myth of a rural monolith of white poverty and social conservativism is wrong. We have dear friends who are immigrants, who are people of color, who are trans and gay, and who have different sets of abilities. We spend our days with so-called bleeding-heart liberals and staunch conservatives alike. Our children have some friends who live with grandparents because their parents are locked in addiction, as well as other friends who own conspicuously fancy homes and take expensive vacations. Every type of variation you see in the country is often visible and compressed within rural communities, where you cannot always attend a different school to separate yourself from differences that might be uncomfortable. We don't pretend that we can speak to all of these multifaceted and complex experiences, but our goal in undertaking this book was to provide a broad survey of rural education—one that looks across the nation at all kinds of rural challenges and makes them plain; and also one that empowers rural practitioners to embrace evidence-based solutions and helps them tailor their efforts in the ways that have proven to be most successful. It is our intention that the book include rich examples and compelling details that will be familiar to education leaders, yet geographically and demographically diverse. Most important, we want rural educators and those who work with them—community leaders, policy makers and funders—to walk away with a more complex understanding of rural schools, and which educational efforts work best.

GUIDING PRINCIPLES

This book not only challenges the presumptions about the bedrock of rural America—its education system and the children it serves—but also presents a framework to understand the complexity of rural education in America. We argue that "rural" is not a binary description that can be determined purely by population size, density, or distance from a major city center. Instead, we need to understand that the rurality (i.e., size, density, geographic distance) of a community interacts dynamically with its wealth and the in-migration/out-migration of its members. For example, a small town in Iowa that has seen an explosion of in-migration when a meatpacking plant opens faces very different issues than a town of the same size in Vermont known for its winter skiing. We then blend research and examples from rural communities across the United States to illustrate effective approaches along the trajectory of a rural student's educational experience from early childhood through postsecondary school. We show how efficacy is determined by the degree to which instruction, interventions, and programs address the needs and strengths of each unique rural community. Efforts that are placed-based, responsive to the current economic needs, and promote collaboration beyond the school walls have the greatest chance of succeeding.

We acknowledge that rural communities have been left out of the dialogue on educational policy and improvement over the last two decades, as much of that discussion has been centered on market-driven approaches that focus on competition as a means to improve school quality. Even reliably measuring student progress year-to-year can be difficult in areas with a small population of students, let alone creating enough demand for charter schools or teachers with higher evaluations. Moreover, we are in an era of data-driven decision making, when very few studies have been conducted on rural students. Rural students have been missing, in part, because we do not capture demographic data with enough nuance to understand the dimensions of rural inequality, and also because the sample sizes are not conducive to statistical analysis. There are many students who are almost completely absent from our empirical knowledge base, including migrant students, rural racial minorities, and rural students with disabilities.

This book also steps away from decades of social science research that has been focused on relocation. We take the stance that rural communities have value, and solutions should fit the sociocultural and historical reality of the community, rather than proposing strategies that fundamentally support out-migration. Moreover, we will address the problematic notion that rural America is simply those left behind after a "brain drain." The notion of brain drain is deeply troublesome, in that it suggests that the only human capital that requires thinking and critical analysis belongs to certain professions associated with a specific type of academic training. Moreover, rural communities need a circulation of talent, so that residents who leave can realistically return and bring their professional training with them, as we did. Very often, those who have left and returned to rural communities are key drivers of community revitalization. It may be an effective strategy to send young adults off for postsecondary education, but with plans and incentives to return home at the right moments in their professional career or personal lives.

Ultimately, we want to take an approach to rural education that is both strengths-based and critical. We will share fifteen years of research that we have conducted in rural communities, much of which is previously unpublished. But because the vast majority of educational research has been conducted in urban centers, we take a grounded approach. That means we incorporate educational research, but also speak to our own experiences and the lived experiences of rural educational practitioners, policy makers, community leaders, and funders. If we are to serve rural communities, we need to take a nuanced approach that fits their sociocultural realities and needs.

HOW TO USE THIS BOOK

This book, first and foremost, is for people like us who choose to live in rural communities and use education as a tool for community development. It is about the type of topics that kept Sky up at night when trying to teach reading to kindergartners and first graders on the Navajo Nation, and about the challenges Geoff faced as a high school administrator who wanted to help his students get to college. But the book is also for a wide array of practitioners. It also touches on the topics Sky works on now, as the director of a program to help first-generation and Appalachian students succeed at the University of the Cumberlands. It is about the issues Geoff faced both when leading a tech start-up and now, in building an entrepreneurial ecosystem to create jobs and opportunity in a rural region where access to broadband and data is limited.

Depending on the lens you take, you may want to read the entire book through, or focus on specific chapters that are most relevant to your work. *Rural Education in America* is organized into three sections: Part I, "The Rural Context," defines what we mean by *rural* and overviews strength and challenges. Part II, "Meeting the Needs of Rural Students," is about successful rural educational initiatives along a cradle-to-career continuum that are especially critical for the future of rural students and their communities. Part III, "Moving to Action," gives strategies and tools for educators who are planning new initiatives and improvement efforts as well as recommendations for policy makers and private philanthropy.

In part I you will find a discussion that will help you understand what is meant by *rural* and the major economic and structural forces that are shaping rural education. Chapter 1 provides a survey of the demographics of rural America today; it also tackles the issue of brain drain and whether or not rural people are moving (or should relocate) to urban clusters. Chapter 2 takes a research-based approach to identifying the strengths of rural communities, including good schools and increased social and economic mobility compared to urban areas. The third and final chapter in part I is about the forces at play in rural communities that shape educational opportunity and needs.

Part II focuses on key issues in rural education that follow a developmental timeline, from early childhood to college and career opportunities. Chapter 4 discusses early childhood education, sharing best practices as well as wrestling with access to and quality of early education and care opportunities in rural communities. Chapter 5 addresses literacy and language development, including that of rural students who speak a language other than English at home. Chapter 6 focuses on science, technology, engineering, and math (STEM) education, including how rural schools can overcome the digital divide and help students imagine themselves in technology careers—even if they have never met someone from that profession. The final chapter in this section discusses college and career access, including innovative models that have narrowed the educational attainment gap in rural communities.

Part III puts ideas into practice. In chapter 8, we provide resources and tools to help readers undertake a self-assessment of their own school or district and identify a challenge to tackle. A cycle of continuous learning is supplied that is specific to rural educational contexts. The final chapter tackles the current way that educational initiatives are rolled out in rural America—including pitfalls and challenges—and then provides guidance for policy. Before making any more investments or policy decisions, we must understand some of the pitfalls of this work and the steps needed to be responsive to the complex educational needs of rural communities.

WHY RURAL EDUCATION MATTERS
NOW MORE THAN EVER

It has never been more critical to pay attention to the unique needs of rural education than now. The divide between rural and urban America exposed in the 2016 election did not happen overnight. It was the result of decades of rapid global and technological change. Over the last fifty years, there has been seismic shift in the global economy, resulting in tremendous negative effects on rural communities in the United States. From 1970 to 2015, the percentage of employment in the US services sector more than doubled, while the proportion of jobs in the predominantly rural industries of agriculture, forestry, fishing, and mining fell more than 50 percent.[4] Rapid technical advances and mechanization in resource extraction exacerbated these job losses. Although the United States made some investments in education, training, and re-skilling in rural communities, these efforts were fragmented, undersized, and, as we will explore more in chapter 9, poorly implemented.[5] The introduction of prescription pain killers in the late 1990s and early 2000s exacerbated the spiraling economic woes of rural communities. Nowhere were these issues more pronounced than in the Kentucky and West Virginia coalfields of Appalachia, where the rapid decline of the coal industry left tens of thousands jobless.

Unemployment in the coal-producing counties of Eastern Kentucky and West Virginia stands well above 10 percent, nearly triple the national average. Even this figure is misleading as it excludes those who are permanently disabled; in these counties more than 20 percent of adults under sixty-five have that designation.[6] The proportion of children living in poverty is above 40 percent. Perhaps most strikingly, people in this region of the United States die eleven years earlier than the average citizen. In every economic report that links quality of life with geography, from the "Opportunity Atlas" dataset to predictors of lifespan to percentage of deaths from opioid overdose, these are some of the hardest hit areas of the country.[7]

After decades of neglect, rural America now faces dual intertwined urgent challenges requiring significant investments in both education and economic development. So, we must not only completely evolve the educational systems in rural America to catch up to the twenty-first century, but also understand what opportunities exist in growing economic sectors that align with the strengths of rural communities. This book directly addresses how to design educational systems in rural America that not only improve academic and social outcomes, but also prepare students for dignified careers that do not force them to leave their home communities.

Now more than ever it is imperative that we make significant educational investments in rural communities. Increasing inequality and the perceived lack of future opportunities have left many people in rural communities justifiably discouraged, angry, and worried—the direct result of which has been social and political destabilization, and policy suggestions that are ever more rigid and polarizing. We have written this book at an unprecedented time in American education, when the Coronavirus pandemic has closed schools across the country and our children finished out the school year at home. Urgent issues such as lack of access to broadband internet now loom as barriers to even the most fundamental educational experiences. We look at our own five-year-old and wonder what kindergarten might look like if schools are still closed in the fall. How will his classmates and friends learn to read? Even more, we are heartbroken to see how the virus has devastated the Navajo Nation, and worry that other rural communities might face this level of devastation. Inequality was already a problem, and we worry deeply about what the future holds. What gives us hope is the rapid way that educators have adapted. We will need all of our creativity and collected wisdom in the years ahead.

We are glad to be tackling these topics in an era when the national mood on rural communities is mixed, and sometimes quite negative. We believe that the first step in healing a rural-urban divide is better understanding. Providing a quality education to all children is a universal value that connects our entire country, whether a person lives in the Massachusetts Bay or among the hollers of the Appalachian Mountains. At the same time, the infrastructure and supports in place for rural communities can be vastly different. Until we begin to better understand the needs of rural communities, our rural schools will continue in the shadows, expected to implement education in a way that was designed for urban realities. We can do better than that. After all, we know from history that our country is the strongest when all groups of people are thriving.

PART I

The Rural Context

1

From the Outside Looking In:
Rural Education Today

WHAT IS RURAL AMERICA LIKE TODAY? In this chapter we provide an overall picture of rural communities and education in the United States, including definitions, demographics, and challenges. In doing so, we will argue that it is impossible to get a true picture of rural life with even the most comprehensive set of statistics and studies, a challenge that has been noted extensively by numerous rural researchers and scholars.[1] Life in a rural community cannot be fully captured empirically, and is often misconstrued and distorted by those who lack this lived experience, most especially the media and many politicians. Indeed, you could describe what it's like to live in a rural community as the recognition that your identity and ways of life are consistently underrepresented and misunderstood in the wider society. We hope that this book will help crack open the ways that rural communities and their schools are presented so that more light may shine.[2] But first, we must begin with the rural milieu of the United States.

One of the most important but misunderstood historical trends concerns the extent to which population in rural communities has declined over the last century or more. For example, in 1800, 94 percent of the US population lived in a rural community.[3] One hundred years later, in 1900, more than 60 percent of the population were still living in rural communities. It was not until the 1920s that more people lived in cities than in small towns or on farms. By 2015, only about 19 percent of the population lived rurally.[4] (See figure 1.1.) However, this seemingly steep decline in the rural population, along with the dramatic increase in urban dwellers, masks some critical facts. That 19 percent of the US population who lived rurally in 2015 was still over sixty million people, including thirteen million children under the age of eighteen.[5] Despite the continued decline in the percentage of people living rurally, there are in fact just about as many people as ever living in rural communities and attending rural schools. (See figure 1.2.)

Rural communities and schools are also more diverse today than ever before in US history. Although rural communities are less racially and ethnically diverse than urban areas, they are not all white, as often portrayed in the media.[6] For example, Hispanics are one of the fastest growing population segments and compose about

FIGURE 1.1   Percentage of rural dwellers has declined, 1900–2015

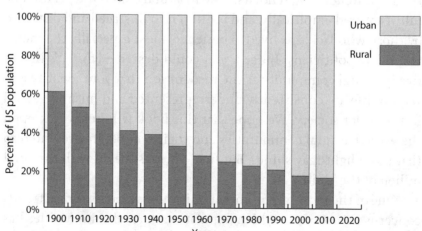

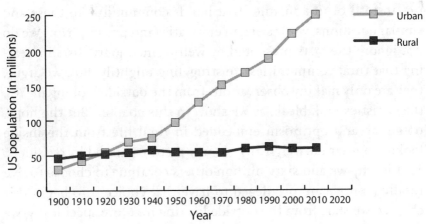

FIGURE 1.2   Number of rural dwellers has stayed steady, 1900–2015

10 percent of people living in rural communities. African Americans and Native Americans constitute 8 percent and 2 percent of the rural population, respectively.

With the changes in the proportion and composition of people living in rural areas come unique challenges. The movement, or agglomeration, of people to urban areas is more a symptom of a struggling rural economy than a sign of a booming urban one. As we discuss later in the chapter, the seismic shift in the world's economy over the past fifty years has disproportionately and negatively affected rural communities. The stressed rural economy has impacted everything from health care to education. A lack of adequate and responsive government and private funding has further exacerbated complex challenges that are now deeply embedded in rural communities. Crumbling and nonexistent infrastructure, poor health outcomes, chronic poverty, and the opioid epidemic are just a few of the seemingly intractable problems that often shape the public narrative.

All of these challenges feed into a larger, overarching question that several *New York Times* articles have recently asked: Should rural communities cease to exist?[7] And more specific to our book: Should schooling be used to educate children away from their communities instead of in a manner that builds community? To these and similar questions, we answer an emphatic (and proud), "No!" We do not ignore the facts presented by well-trained journalists indicating that rural communities are struggling mightily. But, we argue, they are only making observations from the outside looking in. Yes, the statistics look bleak, as we show in this chapter. But the hope, potential, and optimism embedded in rural life from the inside looking out far outweigh any gloomy picture painted by outsiders. That is why we and sixty million others continue to choose to live rurally (and we are privileged to have that choice!). To begin this chapter, we start from the outside looking in. More specifically, we examine the myriad definitions of what is "rural."

DEFINING RURAL

What defines a "rural" community? Does it even matter? For us, a quote from US Supreme Court Justice Potter Stewart about whether a particular film was too obscene to be shown to the public seems apt: "I know it when I see it."[8] It might be as you are traveling out of the city—the subdivisions become sparse and suddenly you are just looking at farm fields, expanses of forest, undeveloped mountains, or wide open ranges. Researchers and government bureaucrats have spent over a century trying to define that exact dividing line where you can confidently say you are now in a rural community.[9] Although it is important to have a working definition of what a rural community is, and we will provide one, we also argue that the challenges and opportunities of ruralness are fluid and cannot be defined by a zip code, census tract, or school district. Defining "rural" should not be used to exclude and isolate. Many consolidated school districts include urban, suburban, and rural communities. For example, Hillsborough County Public Schools in Florida encompasses the urban city center of Tampa, its sprawling subdivisions, and citrus and strawberry farm communities in the east end of the county. The needs of the rural school communities in Hillsborough are salient not only to the families and children living near citrus plantations, but also to the superintendent and executives in their Tampa-based central office. And Hillsborough is not unique: Charlotte-Mecklenburg Schools in North Carolina, Clark County School District in Nevada, and Boulder Valley School District in Colorado all have similar contexts.

At the same time, the reality is that a number of government funding streams depend on strict definitions of what constitutes a rural community. There is no better discussion of the challenges defining "rural" than that provided by Michael Ratcliffe and colleagues at the US Census Bureau in their brief, *Defining Rural at the US Census Bureau*.[10] Their report explains that the rapid industrialization and urbanization of America over the past one hundred years led to a significant decline in the proportion of Americans living rurally. US Census Bureau researchers, who are experts at defining the demography of the United States, started classifying urban and rural communities as early as the 1860s. By the early twentieth century, the Census Bureau had created a dichotomous approach to their classifications.[11] Urban was any community more than 2,500 people; rural was everything else. Over the twentieth century, the definition evolved to consider different settlement patterns and the growth of suburbs. But the fundamental "urban-centric" approach stayed the same—urban was defined first, with all other areas being classified as rural.[12] That the urban definition drives what it means to be rural, at least to the official census takers, isn't all that surprising. This same urban-centric approach is found in everything from educational policy to philanthropic giving.

The Census Bureau's current definition of rural uses a combination of population density, land-use characteristics, and distance to first define an urban area's "footprint." Briefly—without getting too technical—this means that census blocks with population densities of five hundred to a thousand or more people per square mile are generally identified as urbanized areas or urban clusters. Everything else not in this urban designation is considered rural, which accounts for about 20 percent of the US population, or sixty million people.

If this definition leaves you disappointed, confused, or argumentative, you are not alone. Ratcliffe offers Stanley County, South Dakota, as an example of the complicated nature of classifying urban and rural communities. As Ratcliffe points out, in 2013, Stanley County had a population of nearly 3,000, with 2,078 people residing in Fort Pierre, South Dakota, the county's largest population center. Even though 99.9 percent of the county's land area is rural, it was designated as an urban county and lumped in the same classification that includes Los Angeles County, California, and Cook County (Chicago), Illinois. Why? Fort Pierre was included in the urban cluster of the small town of Pierre (population 14,425), just across the Missouri River, and that shifted the proportion of people living in an "urban" area in Stanley County.

We don't want to lose sight of the forest for the trees, but several more derivatives of the US Census Bureau definition of "rural" are important to note because of their ties to funding streams and program evaluation. One from the Office of Management and Budget (OMB), which tracks how federal dollars are spent and to what impact, uses the less precise definitions of "Metropolitan Statistical Areas," urbanized areas of 50,000 or more residents, and "Micropolitan Statistical Areas," which have 10,000 to 50,000 people. However, Metropolitan and Micropolitan Statistical Areas are not synonymous with urban and rural. Yet the OMB is using these inconsistent designations to inform federal budgetary decisions; there are numerous rural counties included in both designations, and many are not included at all![13]

A few federal agencies, such as the US Department of Agriculture (USDA), US Department of Health and Human Services

(HHS), and US Department of Veteran's Affairs (VA), align strictly with the US Census Bureau's definition of rural to fund programs serving those communities. For example, the USDA Rural Development Home Loan program defines rural as nonmetropolitan counties that include a combination of open countryside, rural towns (places with fewer than 2,500 people), and urban areas with populations ranging from 2,500 to 49,999.[14] HHS uses similar criteria for the administration of its Rural Health Grants. For its Office of Rural Health, the VA uses a hybrid of the USDA and HHS models called the Rural-Urban Commuting Areas (RUCA) to define rurality. RUCA's urban designation is a census tract where at least 30 percent of the population lives in an urban area as defined by the Census Bureau; rural is defined as everything else.[15]

RURAL IN EDUCATION

Like the USDA, HHS, and VA, the National Center for Education Statistics (NCES) and its reporting agency, the Institute of Education Sciences (IES), base their definitions of "rural" and "urban" on the Census Bureau definitions. NCES further breaks down urban communities in the United States into three categories: city, suburban, and town. All of these categories fall into either "urbanized areas" with populations of 50,000 or more or "urbanized clusters" of populations between 2,500 and 50,000. Once again, in this urban-centric model, rural areas are defined as everything other than cities, suburbs, or towns.[16] What is most puzzling about this definition is that it includes towns with fewer than 10,000 people and far from a major city as "urbanized clusters." In fact, towns with a population as small as 2,500 are still considered urbanized clusters, and are often categorized in research and policy with much larger urban cities. For anyone living in a small town of fewer than 10,000 people, especially far from a major city, the idea that their community is considered urban by the federal government is absurd.

Unfortunately, this definition is used by the IES, the government agency charged with providing "scientific evidence on which to ground education practice and policy."

Not surprisingly, rural educational researchers have for decades pointed out the flaws and inherent limitations in these urban-centric definitions of rural communities.[17] Howley, Theobold, and Howley; Biddle and Azano; and Tieken have all eloquently and succinctly explained the trouble with first defining urban areas, and then designating rural as what's not urban.[18] They rightly point out that rural communities often cannot be delineated by a census tract or county line, and that being rural is more about a daily lived experience. As Tieken explains:[19]

> It's this feeling—something beyond the size of a population or its proximity to a city—that many rural scholars and advocates feel should actually define rural . . . "Rural," then, is a matter of the commonplace interactions and events that constitute the rural "lifeworld . . ." This understanding, shared by many of the residents of rural communities, is tied to place; it provides a geography-dependent sense of belonging. Rural, in this conception, is not simply a matter of boundaries. It constitutes one's identity; it shapes one's perspectives and understandings; and it gives meaning to one's daily experiences. This identity, this shared and place-dependent sense of rural belonging, gives rural its significance.

Although this definition lacks the strict population criteria adopted by federal agencies, we identify strongly with it, having been born, raised, and lived most of our lives in rural communities. Some of those places would fit any definition of rural, but others might not, depending on the specific designation. Yet we have never questioned whether our home was rural. Obviously, the government needs specific criteria to define "rural" so that funding streams can support programs for rural communities' needs.

But the urban-centric approach does not capture the whole land-scape of rural communities. Indeed, we believe that the census-based definition of "rural" undercounts millions and perhaps tens of millions of people who strongly identify as living in rural communities. The map in figure 1.3 offers three examples of urbanized areas and urban clusters, as defined by the Census Bureau; we know firsthand, having lived in those areas, that dozens of communities identified as "urban" would find the distinction preposterous.[20]

It is true that living rurally encompasses more of a "life-world" that is hard to describe without experiencing it for yourself. Although we are trained academics turned practitioners who are embedded in rural America, we have come to define rurality through another lens that is less rigidly statistical and more balanced and asset-based. We (and any rural resident living in America

FIGURE 1.3   Examples of rural communities classified as urban

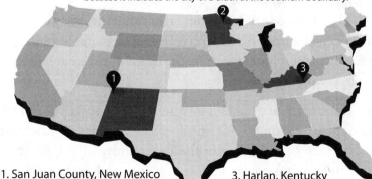

2. Saint Louis County, Minnesota
Saint Louis County stretches from Duluth all the way to Canada. It contains over 900,000 acres of wildlands, and has a population density of 32 people per square mile. The county is 6,860 square miles, but is considered urban because it includes the city of Duluth at the southern boundary.

1. San Juan County, New Mexico
63% of San Jaun County is Native nations; the population density is 21 people per square mile. Residents would have to travel over 180 miles to an airport. It is considered urban because the 5,538 square mile county has one town of 50,000, although no interstate highways.

3. Harlan, Kentucky
The town of Harlan has a population of 1,452 and is the most populous location in the mountainous county. Residents have to travel over an hour to reach an interstate and 3 hours to reach an airport. Harlan is still considered an "Urban Cluster" by the US Census Bureau.

today), for example, might use the following criteria to describe our community:

1. Walmart and Family Dollar are a part of your daily and weekly routine.
2. You gladly travel more than thirty minutes to try out a new restaurant.
3. Introductions are rarely needed, but in the rare case you "meet" someone new, you spend at least five minutes catching up on shared relatives, friends, and maybe what church you attend.
4. You are part of a close-knit community and proud of it.
5. You don't lock the door to your home.
6. You have to drive everywhere.
7. The seasons and weather play a big role in your life.
8. Town sports are life; your entire school district was closed when a team went to the state playoffs.
9. You know people by the cars they drive, and everyone waves at everyone.
10. A high school girl was crowned the town queen during your community's annual festival.
11. You went to school with kids from eight other tiny towns.
12. When people ask you where you are from, you mumble your tiny town's name and then automatically tell them what larger town it is near.

These criteria reflect our lived experience of rural communities. They are based on the defining characteristics of knowing and being known by everyone in the community; living far from amenities; and having common social events and experiences. If you identified with any of these statements, you more likely than not grew up in a community with fewer than twenty-five thousand people and lived more than thirty miles from a city with a population greater than fifty thousand.

This place-based and commonsense definition of rural includes many of the small towns designated as "urban areas" in the Census Bureau definition, and provides a guide for just how many students in the United States live a rural educational experience. Just using the strict Census Bureau definition of rural identifies more than nine million students attending rural schools, more than the nation's eighty-five largest school districts combined.[21] But as we define rural, this is a vast underestimation of the true number of students attending rural schools, a number that may be double. The urban-centric definition of rural has not only undercounted families and children living in rural communities, but also obfuscated many of the hardships these families face. It is only in the last decade that those challenges have become so damaging they cannot be ignored any longer.

CHALLENGES FACING RURAL COMMUNITIES AND SCHOOLS TODAY

The defining characteristics of a rural community—which can be summed up generally as geographic distance from cities and amenities, low population density, deep sense of place, and strong community ties—can create unique problems. With the election of President Donald J. Trump, who captured nearly two-thirds of the rural vote in 2016, there's been increased attention on many of the challenges facing rural America.[22] These include a struggling economy, inadequate government and private funding, lagging infrastructure, and poor health outcomes. We address each of these, not to deviate from our strengths-based lens, but to give you a full picture of rural communities from the outside looking in.

Struggling Economy

The unprecedented globalization and revolution in technology over the past three decades brought tremendous economic growth

globally. However, those gains were not universal; the biggest bene-
factors were people in rapidly developing countries such as China
and India. In the United States, gains in technology and innovation were coupled with concentrated economic growth and higher
paying jobs in "entrepreneurial hubs" located on the coasts and in
large cities across the Midwest and Mountain West.[23] As wealth
and opportunities agglomerated in these urban communities, rural
America was getting left further and further behind.

The forces behind these shifts had actually been in place since
the 1970s and 1980s. Over the last fifty years, there has been a seismic shift in the global economy. From 1970 to 2010, the percentage
of employment in the services sector in the United States more
than doubled, while the proportion of predominantly rural jobs
in agriculture, forestry, and fishing was cut in half.[24] Rapid technical advances and mechanization in resource extraction exacerbated
these job losses in rural communities.[25] As a result, unemployment and poverty in rural communities has skyrocketed; in the
late 1990s about one in five rural counties had a poverty rate higher
than 20 percent. By 2018, this figure had increased to about one in
three rural counties.[26] These statistics do not include the mass out-
migration of rural employable adults. Job growth in cities far sur-
passed that in rural areas, and these so-called agglomeration effects
have been well-documented by researchers.[27] The educational and
workforce development systems could not keep up with the rapid
changes in the economy and dislocation of workers.[28] And at least
one big reason has been the inequitable government and private
philanthropic funding for rural communities.

Unequal Funding

It is well known that rural schools are more expensive to operate
than their urban counterparts. In rural communities, buses travel
great distances to transport children.[29] Schools and districts lack
the economies of scale that give their urban equivalents pricing

power with curriculum, technology, and food vendors. Despite these higher operating costs, formulas for federal funding disproportionately allocate dollars to urban students.[30] Take Title I funding, for example—the largest source of federal funding for public schools. Designed to support academic achievement for disadvantaged students, Title I is often the largest source of discretionary spending for schools where a majority of students qualify for a free or reduced-price lunch.[31] In a complex formula that uses "number weighting" for disadvantaged students and state education spending, Title I funding has been shown to systematically underfund rural schools because it emphasizes the number of children in poverty, not the proportion. The result is that impoverished rural school districts receive far less per pupil in Title I funding than their large urban counterparts, even if the proportion of students living in poverty is the same. One report showed that of the nation's nine hundred poorest rural districts, 797 are underfunded by $54.5 million, an average of more than $68,000 per district.[32] Marty Strange, former director of policy for the Rural School and Community Trust, provides a poignant example of this inequitable funding by comparing the urban Philadelphia, Pennsylvania, school district (population 1.5 million) to the rural Philadelphia, Mississippi, school district (population 7,300). According to Strange, urban Philadelphia, Pennsylvania, receives $2,424 in Title I funding for each of its disadvantaged students, while rural Philadelphia, Mississippi, receives only $1,246 per student.

Attempts to close this gap have been unsuccessful. One attempted fix was proposed in 2012 with the All Children Are Equal Act, but substantive changes were never adopted.[33] The US Department of Education tried to alleviate some of the discrepancy with the Small, Rural School Achievement Program (SRSA) and Rural and Low-Income School Program (RLIS), which gave rural schools access to additional federal funding streams. However, these changes were made through Title V of the reauthorization of the

Elementary and Secondary Education Act, which required school districts to apply for the funds and limited allowable activities.[34] In 2019, the combined programs provided rural school districts across the United States about $100 in additional funding per student, far less than was needed to make up for the Title I funding discrepancies. To put this in perspective, consider that to even qualify for the programs, a school district cannot have an enrollment of more than six hundred students, which eliminates many rural districts. So, on average, a qualifying rural school district might receive an extra $6,000 annually from SRSA and RLIS. At best, this approach allows a number of very small, rural districts to perhaps match the funding of urban schools, but still does not address the fact that rural schools are more expensive to operate. More troubling, the eligibility criteria for the SRSA and RLIS stipulate that all schools in a district must be classified as rural in order to qualify. If just one school in a predominantly rural district is not considered rural, the entire district is disqualified for SRSA and RLIS.[35]

It's beyond the scope of this book to get into the details of complex funding formulas at the state and local levels. But consider that every state allocates funding to some degree based on student enrollment or average daily attendance. Furthermore, in all states education is mostly funded through property taxes. The negative consequences of these funding mechanisms on rural school funding are obvious. The agglomeration of jobs in urban areas forces out-migration of families and their children from rural communities, thus decreasing enrollment and lowering overall funding from the state and federal government. A recent report confirmed these deleterious effects, showing that on average rural school districts receive 17 percent of state education funding, although they serve 20 percent of students.[36] In addition, a struggling economy with out-migration eventually leads to large inventories of real estate, a "buyer's market," and lower property values, which also decreases the tax base for schools. This one-two punch is felt keenly in rural communities across the United States.

It is also harder for rural communities to turn to funding from foundations and wealthy philanthropists.[37] Foundation giving in 2018 was over $75 billion, constituting a tremendous amount of resources.[38] But rural communities, which represent at least 20 percent of the US population, received only about 6 percent of foundation grants.[39] Furthermore, grants from some of the largest private foundations, such as the Bill & Melinda Gates Foundation, Walton Family Foundation, and Annie E. Casey Foundation, funded rural communities at a rate of $88 per capita. In urban areas, these same large foundations gave urban communities more than twice that amount.[40] Nowhere is this disparity clearer than when comparing charitable per capita giving in some of the wealthiest communities to that in some of the poorest. From 2010 to 2014, foundations awarded more than $4,000 in grants per person in San Francisco.[41] During that same time period in rural Appalachian Kentucky and the Lowcountry of South Carolina, total grants awarded came to just $43 per person. The ratio of awards given is staggering; for every $1 a rural organization received in Kentucky or South Carolina, $100 was given to counterparts in San Francisco. Of course, the reasons for the discrepancy are many and complex. Rural communities lack relationships with foundations; funders perceive rural communities as lacking the capacity and infrastructure to handle large grants; there is an overreliance on big numbers, found only in urban areas, to prove efficacy and impact. These may be valid explanations, but the problem of rural-urban inequity remains.

Lagging Infrastructure

Dilapidated roads, crumbling bridges, failing dams, inadequate water treatment, inconsistent electric service, and spotty or nonexistent internet and cell service. These realities of everyday rural life are some of the consistent barriers to providing a quality education. What is interesting is just how much of the overall US infrastructure is located in rural areas. Nearly 75 percent of the entire US transportation system is rural, including 74 percent of bridges and 73 percent of roads.[42] Nearly 95 percent of water treatment facilities in the United States supply communities with fewer than ten thousand persons.[43]

There are numerous examples of how poor and failing infrastructure impedes and burdens rural schooling. For example, a national study on access to basic utilities found rural households were more likely than urban to have been without running water at least once in the preceding three months or to have used a kerosene space heater.[44] In our community in rural Eastern Kentucky, students regularly miss ten to twenty school days a year due to ice and snow on roadways. Lacking proper road-treatment equipment, the mountain roads become deadly with even the tiniest layer of ice or snow. Even more disturbing is the existing and widening digital divide between rural and urban communities. For three years we lived in a remote part of Harlan County, Kentucky, where there was no cell service for a radius of thirty miles around our home. In the community where we live now, with a population of 1,700, it is impossible to obtain consistent cell service for more than a ten-minute drive. Whole swaths of communities go without access to the internet or cell service, and when it is available, it is often inadequate and expensive (e.g., 5 megabits/second download speed for $70/month).

The digital divide between urban and rural communities was identified as early as the 1980s.[45] Even then, before the internet age, researchers and policy makers were asking if the urban-rural digital divide was worsening.[46] We now know it was and continues to do so. According to a recent report from the Federal Communications Commission, 39 percent of the rural population (23.4 million based on the Census Bureau definition of rural), compared to just 4 percent of the urban population, could not access basic fixed broadband service.[47] A full 20 percent of rural America cannot even get service higher than 5 megabits/second.[48] And as many rural residents know, even if they do have access to higher speeds, service is monopolized by one provider and costs significantly more. The bottom line is that more than ten million rural Americans lack access to internet speeds to even stream videos, which are increasingly becoming a core component in twenty-first-century education. It is no surprise, then, that a recent survey found almost a quarter of rural adults identified high-speed internet service as a "major problem" in their community.[49] In chapter 6, which looks at science, technology, engineering, and math (STEM) education efforts, we go into depth about how the digital divide affects rural schools. Just how important this gap is for education came into clear view when the coronavirus pandemic closed schools and the most expedient way to deliver content was through the internet. Many rural schools were forced to improvise, knowing that their students would not have access to the internet speeds required for learning.

Poor Health Outcomes

It was no exaggeration when several news outlets declared that rural America faces a "health-care crisis."[50] People living in rural areas suffer from higher rates of obesity and diabetes.[51] Disability rates are also more prevalent in rural communities.[52] These statistics play out similarly for children; rural children are more likely to be overweight, obese, and have diabetes than urban children, even when controlling for reported exercise and diet.[53] Most striking, mortality rates, adjusted for socioeconomic status, are higher for rural children than for urban children.[54]

These health-related statistics highlight the vast health inequalities that plague rural America. Furthermore, these health disparities were amplified when the opioid epidemic began to ravage rural communities. Indeed, rural America was ground zero for the opioid epidemic.[55] Its devastating effects were known as early as the 1990s in many communities, and they have nearly wiped out an entire generation. In 2017, the epidemic was killing 130 people each day, more than the top five leading causes of death combined.[56] Mostly rural states in the Appalachian coalfields were hit the hardest. West Virginia and Kentucky have led the nation in opioid-related deaths for more than a decade. Such a travesty completely changes the trajectory of entire communities of children. In many rural communities, more than one-third of children are being raised by their grandparents or other guardians because their parents are either actively addicted, incarcerated, in treatment, or deceased.[57] But this also brings in new challenges for schools, which may be the best delivery mechanism of health services for children in their communities. Indeed, the School Superintendent Association includes addressing health barriers and ending food insecurity as two of their five recommendations for how schools can "level the playing field" for rural students.[58]

FROM THE OUTSIDE LOOKING IN: A DYSTOPIAN SOCIETY

When you look at these statistics and challenges together, you may wonder why anyone would want to live in a rural community, let alone send their children to local schools. Here in Appalachian Kentucky, we commonly see reports that our home counties are ranked as the worst places to live in America. And we are not alone. In 2014, a now infamous—at least for rural people—New York Times article listed the top ten "hardest places to live" in the United States.[59] All ten communities were rural—six in Appalachian Kentucky and the remaining four in the rural South, spread across Mississippi, Arkansas, Georgia, and Louisiana. With so many discussions of rural communities focused on the "brain drain" away from rural communities, it may be that outsiders assume that anyone with intelligence and energy has already left. Yet, ours is a country where the vast majority of people live in or close to the community where they grew up.[60] We wonder why it is that we expect, and even encourage, people from rural communities to relocate from their seemingly dismal hometowns when the same would never be true of urban dwellers. But, this is just pondering the perceptions of people looking from the outside into rural communities. We know from our own lived experiences and those of our children that rural communities are places of unique assets and opportunities.

FROM THE INSIDE LOOKING IN: PLACES OF ASSETS AND OPPORTUNITIES

Behind the inspirational words of "hope, potential, and optimism" we offered at the beginning of the chapter there are definable and observable unique assets across rural school communities: a deep sense of place, strong community and kinship bonds, innate understanding and appreciation for the natural world, development of selflessness, and the central role schools play in communities with few other resources. Rural communities also have a protocol of communal independence and resilience that is demonstrated consistently even through economic collapses, natural disasters, and human tragedies.[61]

Importantly, these strengths play out differently across rural schools. As we explain in the next chapter, rural communities and their schools are not homogeneous and not all approaches work equally well. Indeed, rural schools are already at a disadvantage in a context where urban and metropolitan educational needs are the driving force in policy development. That handicap is further exacerbated when policy and pedagogy are designed and implemented inflexibly and uniformly across varied rural educational communities. As anyone knows who has lived, visited, or traveled through rural America—the mountains of Appalachia, cotton fields of the South, Western ranches, Great Plains farms, or any of the numerous Native American reservations—there is great diversity. How do you take the unique strengths of rural schools in these diverse contexts into account when designing programs and instruction that work? In the next chapter, we more deeply examine these rural advantages and what makes rural communities and their schools so special.

2

From the Inside Looking In:
The Strengths of Rural Communities

IF RURAL AMERICA is the new "inner city," as reporters from the *Wall Street Journal* have stated, why do people choose to stay in or return to rural communities?[1] The answer may be perplexing to outside observers who point to data about the relative economic weaknesses and poor health outcomes in rural areas. Before we get into the strengths of rural communities and schools, we will first consider the double standard of residential mobility for rural residents, when those in popular media often suggest rural Americans should just get up and go.[2]

First, let's be clear that adults in the United States overwhelmingly live near the places they grew up, and few people like to relocate. In 2016, the US Census Bureau reported that the number of Americans moving in the past year had fallen to a new low at 11.2 percent.[3] A 2018 Pew report found that not only do most American adults live near their hometown, but 37 percent have never lived outside their hometown and 57 percent have never lived outside of their home state, if time in the military or college is excluded.[4]

Demographic surveys show that the typical adult in the United States lives only eighteen miles from his or her mother.[5]

Valuing the place you are from, prioritizing family connections over wealth, and wanting to be near your roots might seem like old-fashioned values specific to rural communities. But these are widespread American values that hold across all social classes, races, and geographic communities. In fact, a Pew report found that family dramatically outranks wealth or career as the reason that adults stay in their hometown, and that it also is the key source of meaning in their lives.[6] Of course, economic conditions are part of the reason why adults tend to live close to home. The support of family—particularly when dealing with the cost of childcare—makes a bigger difference to families who have less disposable income.[7] In short, it just makes good economic sense. So why would we expect rural residents to leave their hometowns when the general trend across the country is to stay near family? Do the difficulties of rural communities really outweigh the benefits of being near family?

In this chapter, we argue that rural communities offer unique benefits to families, particularly in terms of education and how it shapes the perspectives and outcomes of children. Our goal is to help identify the strengths of rural communities so that we can build on these as we discuss the role of education and how to design effective rural programs.

STRENGTHS OF RURAL COMMUNITIES

Rural communities have real and important strengths. In 2014, Raj Chetty and colleagues published a seminal article on intergenerational social mobility in the United States.[8] While leading research for the Equality of Opportunity Project, Chetty found that communities with high socioeconomic mobility have higher quality K–12 education, more family stability, greater social capital, lower income inequality, and less residential segregation.[9] It was not a great surprise to scholars that these factors were associated with greater economic mobility. What did make headlines when the research came out was that children from rural communities had a better chance at upward mobility than their suburban and urban counterparts.[10] This surprising finding affirmed what many people raising their children in rural communities already knew. Greater socioeconomic and racial integration; strong, deep, and stable social networks; and excellent schools were qualities more often found in rural communities than urban ones.

Subsequent research underscored the impact on upward mobility that living in a rural community has for children. Using the same data on social mobility, Bruce Weber and a team of researchers at Oregon State University found that it was the distance to a metropolitan area that most affected upward mobility in rural communities.[11] Rural communities closer to cities actually had worse upward mobility than those farther away. This finding suggests that if you want your children to have the best shot at the American Dream, living better off than their parents and grandparents, it may be better to live farther from large urban areas.

Of course, there are exceptions, which popular media often holds up as the universal rural American experience. But overall, the more rural your community, the more likely your children will have a better life than your own. These and other studies on social mobility began to finally crack the black box of what it means to live and go to school in a rural community. Most importantly, they begin to unpack the positives of living rurally.

We now take a closer look at the strengths of rural communities identified by Chetty and others: greater socioeconomic and racial integration; strong, deep, and stable family ties and social networks; and excellent schools. We also highlight one strength often found in rural communities that is not captured in the mobility data—a greater connection to the natural world and traditional foodways.

FIGURE 2.1   Strengths of rural communities

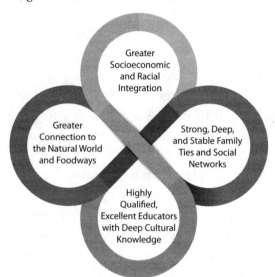

Greater Socioeconomic and Racial Integration

On almost any socioeconomic measure, living standards in rural communities are more equal than urban ones.[12] The disparities found in urban communities just do not exist in rural ones. Rural areas do not have the wide range of wealth found in urban communities, which are often home to some of the richest and poorest people in the United States. The distribution of wealth in rural communities is more compressed and home ownership rates are much higher.[13]

Furthermore, it is difficult for the rural wealthy to segregate themselves from the rural poor as urban residents might do with gated communities, luxury condominiums, upscale shopping centers, and high-end organic grocers. In a rural community, you might be able to build a five-thousand-square-foot house with a swimming pool on ten acres of land. However, more than likely a few single-wide trailers or dilapidated homesteads abut your property.

The rural wealthy not only have neighbors who are less well off, but they also shop at all the same stores, visit the same doctors, and importantly, attend the same schools. Parity is strongly embedded in rural health-care and educational systems. Most rural communities have only a handful of family practitioners and even fewer dentists. The rich and poor alike see the same health-care providers at the same clinic or hospital (if one even exists).[14]

Their children also attend the same schools. It is very difficult for rural families to use inherited or earned wealth to move into a desirable attendance zone so their children can go to a school with real or perceived higher quality. The geographic distance between schools, and the fact that most rural elementary and middle schools feed into one consolidated high school, mean that all children in a rural community—poor or rich—are attending similar schools in the same school system. Moreover, the schools across rural communities are also fairly equal. The top five states with the most equitable statewide school funding distribution are all largely rural (in order of rank): Alaska, Utah, Minnesota, Wyoming, Nebraska, and South Dakota.[15]

As recent research shows, schools across America today are as segregated now as they were fifty years ago.[16] In suburban areas, segregation is especially pronounced. The average African American or Latino student in a suburban area attends a school that is more than 75 percent nonwhite, whereas white suburban students enroll in schools with fewer than one-third minority populations.[17] Segregation is certainly a real problem in some rural communities.[18] However, on the whole, rural schools are more racially integrated than many would expect, even when you consider that these communities are home to a much smaller proportion of nonwhite students than urban areas.[19] In addition, rural communities, where resource extraction plays a critical role in the economy, often rely on immigrant and migrant labor, who are typically people of color. The meatpacking plants in Iowa, poultry processors in Georgia, apple orchards in Eastern Washington, and vegetable growers in rural California all rely on people of color, largely Hispanic, to operate. These workers' children attend local schools. Even where we live in Eastern Kentucky, which is largely white, there are significant numbers of African Americans who settled in the region decades ago to work in the coal mines, as well as African and Asian immigrants who work in health care and Latino immigrants who operate successful businesses.

The benefits of this socioeconomic and racial integration are multifaceted and well proven. First, children who attend schools that are more economically and racially integrated have higher academic achievement. They score higher on nationally normed tests and are less likely to drop out of high school.[20] Being a member of a community and attending school with people different from yourself also improves critical thinking, problem solving, and creativity.[21] These advantages endure throughout life as well. Attending a more economically and racially diverse school reduces bias and enhances leadership skills.[22] More-integrated communities and schools are also better at providing more equitable access to resources and opportunities.[23]

There is no question that rural communities have a long way to go to be fully accepting of the diversity of experiences represented by student populations. Social problems such as racism are real and ongoing. We do not mean to suggest that rural communities have solved issues of inequality, but rather to recast social and economic integration from a deficit of rural schools to a real opportunity to make change and improve student lives. In one of the most thorough studies on rural education and community well-being, Cynthia Duncan found that the rural communities and schools that embrace social mobility have the best outcomes.[24] But perhaps one of the most compelling examples comes from bell hooks, an African American author and activist who has written a moving account of how her experiences of racism in rural Kentucky were far less than many urban people would expect, and how people in cities were often dismissive when she told them about the open dialogue around race that can occur in rural communities.[25] In *Teaching to Transgress*, hooks speaks directly of the opportunities schools can create:[26]

> The academy is not paradise. But learning is a place where paradise can be created. The classroom with all its limitations remains a location of possibility. In that field of possibility we have the opportunity to labour for freedom, to demand of our-selves and our comrades, an openness of mind and heart that allows us to face reality even as we collectively imagine ways to move beyond boundaries, to transgress. This is education as the practice of freedom.

We have seen that possibility in the rural schools our children attend, where they are in classes with a very diverse mix of peers, from children who are uncertain about where they will sleep to those whose parents are doctors and lawyers. In these settings, children and their families have no choice but to deeply under-stand the lives of others who are different from themselves. There is no echo chamber; conflicting ideas, values, and experiences are continually expressed. Some are resolved and others not. And that interaction with people from different backgrounds is amplified thanks to the embedded family and social networks inherent in every rural community.

Strong, Deep, and Stable Family Ties and Social Networks

There is a preponderance of research describing the strong, deep, and stable family ties and social networks in rural communities.[27] These social connections are often embedded in decades or even centuries of intermarriages, business partnerships, celebrations, and tragedies. Although these close ties have tremendous benefits, it is important to acknowledge drawbacks. Books like *Main Street* by Sinclair Lewis and *Devils* by Fyodor Dostoevsky provide engaging and often accurate satirical critiques of small-town rural life where everyone is connected and gossip is a daily form of entertainment. For those who are different or do not follow established community norms, breaking those ties can amplify the feelings and experiences of isolation.[28] There are also significant challenges for professionals, who must balance the privacy of their clients or patients with the other roles they serve in a community. These "dual relationships" in rural communities are often difficult to manage and maintain as people navigate multiple roles and touchpoints, beyond their day job.[29]

Yet these deep and stable ties and networks can have significant positive benefits. Schools in rural areas serve as centers of the community.[30] Supplementary social service programs such as grocery backpacks, Christmas present aid, clothing, jackets, dental care, eye care, and vaccinations already operate through most rural schools. Schools have also become the primary provider for mental health services, especially in rural communities where there are few providers and geographic distances inhibits access.[31]

Rural educators' lives intersect with those of their students in multiple ways beyond the classroom. Schools are often the first to know and mobilize when a student and his/her family needs support. The strong networks that form between schools and the community enhance collaboration between other agencies and organizations. For example, social service agencies in rural communities rely exclusively on schools for need identification, service deployment, and follow-up.[32] They will often direct requests for services through the schools' educators, nurses, and counselors to triage and allocate limited resources.

The bureaucratic processes that often plague larger urban schools are ameliorated because the people responsible for service or resource deployment already know the necessary background information on the student, family, and situation. When a need arises, the person directly responsible for delivering a resource or service is notified. When that help is not readily available, appeals are made directly to community members and faith-based organizations. Consider, for example, what happens when a family is in crisis. Here in Eastern Kentucky flooding and house fires are a regular occurrence. Before the flood waters recede or the fire is fully extinguished, the community—typically led by educators and school leaders—has secured emergency housing, clothing, food, and other needed resources for the families involved. Children affected by the tragedy are often in school the very next day. Indeed, at no time are the strength and stability of family ties and community networks more apparent than when a disaster strikes a rural community.

There are many examples of rural communities hit hard by tornadoes, floods, hurricanes, or wildfires. Sometimes, the disaster and subsequent response are so catastrophic that the ties and networks are ripped apart, destroying communities and their schools. Take the Buffalo Creek flood disaster in Logan County, West Virginia, in 1972. On the night of February 26, a coal slurry pond burst, spilling 132 million gallons of wastewater down the mountain, wiping out sixteen rural coal camp towns, killing 125 people and injuring 1,121.[33] The flood also left more than four thousand people homeless. In response, the state and federal government hastily put up emergency housing with no regard for the family and community connections in each of the sixteen small towns. The result, chronicled by Yale sociologist Kai T. Erikson in an award-winning book, *Everything in Its Path*, was complete destruction of all the communities.[34] The haphazard resettlement ripped apart families and the support networks upon which they relied. This loss of what he termed "communality" had devastating effects far beyond the disaster itself, including significant increases in alcoholism, drug abuse, suicide, divorce rates, and depression.[35] Erikson explains the importance of communality in rural communities: "It can offer a place, a rhythm, a coherence. It can protect one from contamination, help absorb the pressures of life, and serve as a source of meaning and energy. When that insulation is stripped away, most people are exposed and alone, and their own bodies become the tissue, as it were, on which disturbances in the surrounding world are recorded in painful detail."[36]

Yet it is often only through the lived experience—from the inside looking in—that you can see how the multiple points of connection and intersecting spheres of influence in rural communities defragment typically siloed services in education, health, and economic development.

Interestingly, some rural education scholars have pointed out that current educational policies undermine the interdependence of relationships in rural schools.[37] They argue that accountability-based testing, uniform curricula, and charter schools emphasize individualized development in the context of a global labor market.[38] It's unclear to what extent these reforms have loosened the ties between communities, families, and students.[39] From our vantage point, these connections are incredibly strong and resilient. One reason why we feel confident that rural schools will always remain tightly interconnected to their communities is that the educators who work there are standout teachers as well as community leaders.

Highly Qualified Educators with Deep Cultural Knowledge

Many people, including our own parents and mentors, questioned our decision to move to Eastern Kentucky from Massachusetts. One of their biggest concerns was the well-being of our children and the quality of education they would receive. However, Sky had spent years studying literacy in the region, and the quality of schooling was actually the least of her worries. As she had discovered through her research, educators and schools in Eastern Kentucky and across rural communities in the United States are some of the very best in the nation. For example, if using state or nationally normed test scores as a proxy, rural schools consistently outperform those in urban and suburban communities.[40] Here in Eastern Kentucky, the results are even more startling. Students in high-poverty schools, where more than 80 percent qualify for a free or reduced-price lunch, score at the national average in reading and math on the National Assessment of Educational Progress.[41] Indeed, research has shown that rural schools are disproportionally better for low-income students.[42] This finding is true for minority immigrants as well. In a recent study about the experiences of Latino immigrants in Arkansas, researchers found that rural schools led to greater social and cultural integration for children. In the rural communities in which they settled, families and their children were able to cross traditional boundaries and increase their economic power.[43]

One reason students do so well in rural schools is straightforward—they have highly qualified teachers. Why there is a concentration of great instructors in rural schools is a bit more complicated and tied to the economic vitality of a community. In many rural communities, the school system is one of the largest employers. It often provides the best-paying jobs with ample benefits and great working conditions, even though on average rural teachers get paid less than those in cities. As many rural scholars have pointed out, schools are inextricably tied to rural development.[44] Teaching is also one of the best career options for students who choose to pursue a bachelor's degree and want to live in their hometown. The result is that rural schools attract some of the brightest former students as teachers; they also have teachers with more years of experience and a smaller proportion of inexperienced teachers than the average US school.[45] In addition, rural schools have a higher percentage of teachers with a full state certification for their subject area.[46] Furthermore, rural and small-town high schools report fewer teacher vacancies and difficult-to-staff positions than their city counterparts.[47]

We should note, however, that rural schools, like their urban peers, still have challenges recruiting teachers for particular subjects, such as special education, math, and science.[48] And some researchers have argued that rural teachers are actually less qualified because a smaller percentage (41.9 percent) have a master's degree than the average US teacher (48.1 percent).[49] We counter these perspectives with the actual performance of students in rural schools and the numerous studies that have shown having a master's degree has no effect on student learning.[50] Furthermore, proximity to a university is a much larger driver of postbaccalaureate degree attainment, and rural counties are home to only 14 percent of the nation's campuses, despite covering 97 percent of the land area.[51]

There's one more very important strength of the rural teaching force. Because rural teachers are often from their school's community, they have a high degree of cultural knowledge. Several studies have emphasized the importance of cultural competence in education, especially in how teachers set expectations for their students.[52] In addition, a long line of rural books has emphasized the need for pedagogy to be closely connected to the needs of rural communities. Perhaps the most well known and popular are the books in the Foxfire series, begun in the early 1970s by a pioneering rural educator, Eliot Wigginton, who allowed students to create their own way to achieve learning standards by designing projects that documented traditional folkways.[53]

Shirley Bryce Heath's seminal 1983 book *Ways with Words: Language, Life, and Work in Communities and Classrooms* brought together sociology and teaching experience to shine a light on small-town and rural life in the South, and how the ways that literacy was used at home and at work transformed the relevance of teaching in the schools.[54] Heath brought race into the discussion, helping clarify that life for the white people in the books was far different than it was for their African American neighbors. This theme has resounded in work that has taken a deep dive into the needs of specific rural communities. For example, in *A Place to Be Navajo: Rough Rock and the Struggle for Self-Determination in Indigenous Schooling*, Teresa McCarty chronicles the painful history of education on the Navajo Nation and how one community reimagined school to meet the needs of their children, particularly preservation of the native language.[55] In *Worlds Apart: Why Poverty Persists in Rural America*, Cynthia Duncan takes this work a step further by contrasting three different rural communities to demonstrate how inequality can undermine community development.[56] All these examples illustrate how enhanced cultural congruence between educators and students in a rural community can strengthen pedagogy and improve learning.

Greater Connection to the Natural World and Foodways

In an era where children ages eight to eighteen spend an average of seven hours a day in front of a digital screen, being deeply connected to the natural world is becoming less common.[57] Recently popular books like *Last Child in the Woods*, *Balanced and Barefoot*, and *The Call of the Wild and Free* have emphasized the importance of being outside and the negative effects of an increasingly digitized world.[58] Today, children spend only half as much time outside as their parents did, and the barrier is often lack of access to safe outdoor green spaces.[59] The consequences have been grim. Since the 1970s, the percentage of children and youth ages two to nineteen who are obese has tripled, and some researchers believe that the brains of children today are being completely rewired.[60] For children in rural communities, the natural world and foodways are a part of everyday life (rain or shine). As many scholars have pointed out, rural communities, their social connections, and ultimately their schools emerge from a deep sense of place and connection to the land.[61] In the twenty-first century, that connection to the land is dwindling for many urban and suburban children. For rural children, lack of access to the internet but an abundance of outdoor play space is at times a benefit.

The important role of nature in giving purpose, independence, and skill is something that rural scholars have long explored. Howley and Howley call these skills "self-provisioning," and discuss how many rural communities find ways to celebrate the resourcefulness that emerges across generations in solving problems by relying on nature.[62] And bell hooks wrote extensively about the fact that nature connects people in ways that can transcend the divides of race and social class.[63] In this way, nature becomes a resource that is abundant to rural schools, and opens up entirely new avenues of valuing students and engaging communities. Because farming and hunting are often part of a region's history and culture, nature becomes a way to respect and value these important elements of students' lives. Perhaps at their best, connections to the natural world and traditional foodways can even help us expand students' identities. For example, Sky and her sister, Sunshine Brosi, once helped female undergraduates see themselves as scientists by pointing out the important role of science in the way that Appalachian women have gathered herbs and used them for healing.[64]

In this chapter, we described the strengths of rural communities. We explained that their scale, in which everyone goes to the same schools, sees the same doctors, and shops at the same stores, fosters integration and deep community and family ties. This social cohesion is a great strength and supports resilience. We explored the role of educators as leaders in the community, and the fact that they not only provide high-quality instruction but also collaborate with other leaders to support children and families. Finally, we suggest that rural communities have a special connection to the natural world. Though rural communities are facing unprecedented difficulties, building on and enhancing these strengths can support the resilience of these communities. In the next chapter, we will look at some of the forces at work in rural communities and how they contribute to rural communities' strengths.

3

The Forces Shaping
Rural Education

WE HAVE EMPHASIZED four key strengths of rural communities. Not all these strengths are present in every rural school community, nor do they appear to the same degree. As many researchers have shown, communities are complex and dynamic, with multifaceted power structures embedded in the culture, history, and geography of an area.[1] Furthermore, who settles in a community and why deeply shapes the values and culture of future generations.[2] Indeed, the social, cultural, and economic history molds every aspect of a community, most especially the structure and form of schooling. Embedded in that sociocultural economic milieu are dynamic factors that shape daily interactions. We will show how these can be used as a framework that every educator and community leader should consider as they design, implement, and evaluate curriculum, instruction, interventions, and programs.

These forces, present in every rural community, not only mediate the strengths described in chapter 2, but they also significantly shape educational efforts and programs. Three of these—population

FIGURE 3.1   Forces shaping rural education

stability, economic vitality, and community leadership—are the
focus of this chapter (see figure 3.1). These elements are drawn from
decades of sociological research on community dynamics, as well
as our own research and practice in the rural communities where
we have lived and worked. They are not all-encompassing and do
not capture every dynamic and interaction that shapes a community's schools, students, and families. However, as we illustrate, how
these forces play out in a rural community can determine the success or failure of educational efforts designed with the very best of
intentions.

Population stability considers the volatility of a community's
residents. Distinct from but closely tied to economic vitality, large
population swings—up or down—are amplified in rural communities. Rural schools can easily become overwhelmed and stressed
with the increase or decrease of only twenty students, let alone one
hundred fifty, as we'll see happened in Postville, Iowa.

The economic vitality of a community captures metrics such as
unemployment rates and median household income; it also includes
the industry mix and availability of job opportunities. As we discuss,
economic vitality significantly shapes whether—or when—students

feel they can return home after college or training. Economic vitality also heavily influences postsecondary attainment.

The third force, community leadership, impacts all communities, rural or urban. Yet it is amplified in rural communities, where schools are central civic organizations and partnerships are based squarely on the individual leader's capacity. Importantly, all three elements are embedded in the social, cultural, and economic history of each community. Without knowing how the past continually shapes the future in rural communities, it is impossible to understand whether these forces will augment or constrain schools and student performance.

Every rural school community is unique. Yet, some powerful lessons can be drawn in comparing how these forces are similar or different across communities. These influences may be present in cities and suburbs as well, but they have a disproportionate effect in rural communities. And they also illustrate why urban-centric educational reform is at the crux of many disconnects in rural education. After all, much educational reform is not as relevant in rural communities, such as a focus on measurement in areas without sufficient population to allow rigorous statistical analysis between cohorts of students or subgroups; a focus on competition in areas that cannot support multiple schools or that struggle to find enough teachers; or a focus on science, technology, engineering, or math (STEM) in areas that cannot offer careers in STEM nearby.

The purpose of this applied framework is specifically for rural practitioners to examine key features of their community so they can critically analyze whether an educational approach or intervention fits their needs. They can make a clearer connection to actionable steps for rural practice that are based on a more nuanced understanding of the needs of the community. For example, consider how population stability shapes early childhood education. In rural farming communities with a stable population, creating a teaching pipeline for young mothers by offering positions within early care centers and schools makes great sense as a way to better connect education with community development: young mothers access greater education and employment opportunities along the way as their children access early learning experiences. But in rural coal mining communities, where the populations have decreased by 20 percent or more in each census for nearly a century, there are often simply not enough early care centers or possible teaching positions to warrant this approach. Instead, a model of combining multiple ages and engaging otherwise isolated caretakers in programming makes far more sense. By having a clear grasp of population trends within their community, practitioners can make better decisions on how to address a need—in this case, early educational experiences—in their specific community.

This is just one example to illustrate how these forces—population stability, economic vitality, and community leadership—shape educational efforts and programs in rural communities. We now describe each in detail and how they are embedded in the social, cultural, and economic history of a community.

POPULATION STABILITY

The population stability of a rural community is intertwined with yet distinct from its economic vitality. Fluctuations in population lag the health of an economy and are shaped by multiple factors beyond economic opportunity. Rural communities by definition have smaller populations spread out over larger geographic areas. The inflow and outflow of families and students matter more in rural areas because schools simply cannot easily adjust to large fluctuations in population. Consider the impact on the school system when a large meatpacking plant in Postville, Iowa (population 2,200) opened up and hired six hundred new workers, a majority of whom were Indigenous Mayan immigrants from Guatemala with few ties to the community. Addressing the educational needs for so many new students, let alone those speaking a different home language, would challenge any school system. But in Postville, where the entire school system enrolls only about six hundred students, the impact was enormous. New teachers had to be hired, classroom space secured, student evaluations conducted, and interpreters found. The school system was solely responsible for educating the families and students about how the US public school system worked.

Then, years later in 2008, once the school system had implemented many of the systems and processes to meet the students' needs, everything changed in one day. Immigration and Customs Enforcement (ICE) conducted the largest raid in US history, arresting four hundred undocumented workers at the Postville meatpacking plant.[3] Nearly all were eventually deported after serving five-month prison sentences. The impact on the schools was immediate and massive; children of plant workers attending school on the day of the raid observed the helicopters circling the plant, thinking the National Guard must be trying to attract new recruits. Then their parents and relatives weren't home when they returned from school. The next day more than one hundred fifty students in the six-hundred-student district were absent. Like most rural communities faced with such a crisis, the school system, along with local churches, served as the safety net and central support system. For months following the raid, the school provided counseling services, recruited translators from a local college, and found professionals—lawyers, doctors, and immigration experts—to ensure students' needs were met. One teacher in the district described their response:[4]

Teachers debriefed in their classrooms with kids so students could better understand the situation, be able to communicate feelings and do away with certain misconceptions they may have had. Students of all backgrounds had worries and questions they would voice. The staff and administration met and collaborated together to discern how to appropriately answer questions and be a support for the students so that all students were getting a consistent message from the staff.

The opening and sudden closing of the meatpacking plant shifted the population of Postville dramatically, putting incredible stress on the local school system. After the plant closed school enrollment dropped significantly, a decline that lasted years. The downward population swing also had devastating effects on the local economy: a number of businesses closed, and dozens of houses went into foreclosure.

Although Postville may seem like an extreme example of population swings, it illustrates how a huge increase or decrease in the number of families and children in a rural community shapes schools and ultimately daily instruction. There are numerous other examples of how population stability (or instability) affects rural communities and schools. In the coalfields of Appalachia, a decades-long decline in population has left school systems doing more with fewer resources to educate students, even as poverty rates increased. With a decreasing enrollment and tax base, many communities are forced to close and consolidate schools. As scholars have pointed out, closing a school means removing the central point of social connectedness that rural schools provide.[5]

Rural communities in states with large seasonal influxes of Hispanic migrant farm labor—California, Washington, Texas, Florida, Oregon, and North Carolina—experience a different, but equally powerful, impact from population swings. Children of migrant farm workers face language and cultural barriers when entering school.[6] Also, they are often at the school for only a short time, during a harvest season. As children grow older, they face increasing pressure to work in the fields, leaving little time for schooling. Many would be surprised at the minimal protections for child workers in the US agricultural sector. Federal law allows ten-year-old children to be hired on farms operated by nonrelatives for short periods of time; twelve-year-olds can work outside school hours with parental permission; and by age sixteen children can do farm jobs, including hazardous ones.[7] The federal government established a Migrant Education Program to assist rural schools educating the identified three hundred thousand migrant farm children in the United States.[8] Funds of approximately $374 million are distributed to states, providing about $1,000 per migrant student each year.[9] Unfortunately, the money is insufficient to combat a high school dropout rate that ranges from 45 to 60 percent.[10]

We find another example of how population stability shapes educational efforts in a rural community with the shale oil boom that began in western North Dakota in the mid-2000s. Facilitated by high oil prices and new drilling technologies, companies began extracting previously inaccessible oil, creating thousands of new jobs in remote sections of North Dakota. Populations boomed, doubling the size of some small rural communities in less than five years.[11] The rapid population increases significantly impacted elementary schools as bulging enrollments put facilities at capacity and exacerbated teacher shortages.[12] Portable classrooms, daily enrollment fluctuations, and housing shortages disrupted instruction and put incredible strain on teachers and administrators.[13] Schools also experienced a marked increase in student mobility as students switched schools when parents received new job assignments.[14]

It goes without saying that the population stability of a rural community has ripple effects that go far beyond the classroom walls. There are longer-term effects on the family ties, social networks, and growth of a rural community. Although a distinct force, population stability is intricately coupled with a rural community's economic vitality, which we look at next.

ECONOMIC VITALITY

Over the last forty years, rapid technological expansion and globalization have put tremendous pressure on the economies and educational systems of rural communities. How a rural community responds to these seismic shifts significantly impacts its economic vitality. Economic vitality encompasses more than traditional financial well-being indicators such as unemployment and poverty rates, median household income, and average home values. It includes the diversity of industry, labor force participation, job-type mix, and the condition of critical infrastructure.[15] All of these factors combined help determine the economic vitality of a community and how it shapes educational systems.

For example, we can see the rippling effects that a relatively straightforward component of economic vitality—the percentage of working-age adults employed—has on a rural school. In Eastern Kentucky, the official unemployment rate ranges from 6 to 12 percent, which is two to three times the US average. However, adults receiving disability or other forms of permanent government support are excluded from these numbers. The actual percentage of adults employed in the region hovers around 40 percent. More than half of all adults aged twenty-five to sixty-four do not have jobs. As many researchers have shown, having a job provides structure to a day and models attitudes and behaviors about work to children.[16] When a large proportion of adults have little structure in their day, their children suffer the consequences. Daily routines such as bedtimes, mealtimes, and hygiene are disrupted. Children in families where no adults have a job struggle with more than just poverty; they have erratic sleep schedules, earlier exposure to inappropriate adult content and language, and poorer health outcomes.[17] When a community has large numbers of nonworking adults, the effects on children can be devastating. Teachers struggle with everything from keeping children awake and focused to combating pessimistic perspectives about the value of education.

Indeed, the economic vitality directly impacts students' beliefs and behaviors toward educational attainment, future job opportunities, and whether to stay or leave their rural community.[18] For decades, the dominant narrative in rural communities at the intersection of economic vitality and education has been the concept of "brain drain," or the idea that promising young adults leave rural communities to find better opportunities in cities.[19] Indeed, a great deal of current research in rural education focuses on how higher education is often positioned by educators as a means of enabling promising students to leave their home communities. In *Learning to Leave*, Michael Corbett follows the economic rise and crash of a small coastal town in Nova Scotia, and the effect on the school system and student outcomes. Corbett concludes that the school system plays a significant role in sorting students and encouraging out-migration.[20] In *Hollowing Out the Middle*, sociologists Patrick Carr and Maria Kefalas studied the educational system's effect on out-migration in a Midwestern community. They grouped children into three categories based on teachers' future expectations. The "Achievers" were college-bound and unlikely to return to the community; "Stayers" came from lower-income families and did not pursue postsecondary education. A third group of "Seekers" did not have as many financial resources as the Achievers, but still sought to leave the community through military service or other means.[21]

It is clear that the rural communities studied in these two books experienced significant out-migration, particularly of students pursuing careers requiring a college education. However, in our opinion, the authors confound the causes of the so-called brain drain and then apply the resulting out-migration universally to all rural communities. In our experience living, teaching, studying, and raising our family in rural communities, the "brain drain" is a direct result of the community's economic vitality. It is not because, as outside researchers often claim, teachers and the school system actively sort and select students to push out of the community. Indeed, it is absurd to believe that rural educators, many of whom are from the community in which they teach, would encourage the best and brightest to leave and not return.

In fact, our experience is quite the opposite. Nearly everyone in the rural communities we know want their children to return. But the biggest barrier is the community's economic vitality, and whether the "Achiever" or "Leaver" can find a job back home. This should not be a surprise, given that the vast majority of people end up living where they grew up![22] What has scholars mixed up about the "brain drain" is that the shift in the US economy over the past four decades has had a disproportionate negative effect on the economic vitality of rural communities.

Indeed, other scholars studying the "brain drain" found no evidence that rural educators actively sorted students and encouraged high performers to leave. Instead, as Schafft and colleagues point out, the economic vitality of a community was the biggest factor determining out-migration.[23] Students who anticipated leaving and not returning did not think there would be jobs available that fit the skills they were pursing after high school.

This is not to say that rural educators tell all their students to stay in the community and never leave. Quite the contrary, teachers in rural communities with all types of economies—declining and improving— encourage their students to go "out in the world."[24] Not surprisingly, this is the exactly the same kind of advice given to students in urban and suburban settings. The reasoning is simple—leave to gain independence, skills, knowledge, ideas, and a larger worldview; then bring those experiences back to your home community. This "boomerang" effect of leaving and returning is prevalent in communities with healthy economies.

Indeed, when the shale oil boom hit North Dakota, communities soon saw the generations that had just left return home to fill the open job opportunities.[25] But North Dakota is not alone, and it may not take a dramatic increase in opportunities to bring adults back to their rural roots. Recent data about the boomerang effect in rural Minnesota found that the population of adults thirty to forty-nine years old has been steadily increasing.[26] The returners are well educated with significant skills and networks, and are seeking a simpler life, lower cost of living, outdoor recreation, and quality schools. The same thing is happening on a much larger scale in India, one of the biggest winners of globalization in the twenty-first century. From 2007 to 2017, nearly 271 million people were lifted out of poverty in India; the percentage of people with electricity increased from 70 percent to 93 percent; access to basic sanitation went from 40 percent to 99.45 percent.[27] With greater economic opportunity and improved infrastructure, many Indians returned to more rural communities to take part in the economic transformation.

The coronavirus pandemic in 2020 only accelerated the trend of people leaving cities and returning to their more rural hometowns. Forced to create home offices in their small apartments, residents in places such as Chicago, New York, and San Francisco questioned the need to live in a densely populated city to work.[28] Indeed, in a poll of two thousand adults living in cities, nearly 40 percent said the coronavirus has made them consider moving to a rural area.[29] Experts believe that the pandemic will continue to reshape cities as remote work becomes normalized and companies allow people to work from anywhere.

It is clear that the economic vitality of a community has a strong and long-lasting effect on the educational trajectory of students and whether they choose to stay, leave, or return. It is also important to note that the educational requirements for the types of opportunities available in a rural community also matter greatly. The coal mining industry is one of the best examples of how a job's education and skill requirements shape educational attainment. Before the recent rapid decline of coal, a high school graduate could begin working in a mine with a starting pay of $60,000. Not surprisingly, many students were drawn to a great-paying job close to home, despite the inherent dangers of mining and volatility of the industry. Local high-paying jobs for high school graduates strongly diminish students' postsecondary educational goals.[30] In several counties in Eastern Kentucky, for example, the percentage of adults with a bachelor's degree or higher is 15 percent compared to the US average of 30 percent, a gap that makes Central Appalachia the US region with the lowest educational attainment.[31] These are just a few examples of how the economic vitality of a rural community shapes its educational system. We'll see this force in more detail when discussing educational efforts in science, technology, engineering, arts, and math (STEAM) as well as college and career readiness in chapters 6 and 7, respectively.

COMMUNITY LEADERSHIP

A long line of research shows how strong civic organizations enhance social well-being.[32] In rural areas, schools already play an oversized role in the community when compared to their urban counterparts. The strengths of schools and their leaders in rural areas, therefore, have an impact far beyond the walls of the classroom. Daily, they shape the economy, health, and resiliency of a community.

Because rural communities do not have the scale to support multiple layers of administration, the efficacy of an organization is determined by the individual capacity of a few key leaders. Indeed, when rural organizations work together or partner on a project, they are doing so more with an individual than an organization. In our work in Kentucky, we see close up the consequences of exceptional versus incompetent (and at times, criminal) heads of organizations. When a leader is extraordinary, everyone stands in line to partner with his or her organization. When they are not, leaders in other organizations will refuse to partner. When a particular kind of organization is desperately needed, but the existing one is hamstrung by incapable, even corrupt, leaders, rural communities will develop entirely new organizations as workarounds. That is one reason why in some rural communities you will find multiple economic development boards, tourism commissions, and even school systems.

And the effect of a poor leader can be long-lasting, especially if the governing board does not hold its executives accountable. One way this plays out in schools is role switching: there are typically only a handful of key leaders in the school system, and the superintendent or principal may not always be among them. It is at times a ranking administrator who has multiple responsibilities. These few leaders are then selective about the organizations they partner with in the community. Most often, their selectivity is not about the work or mission of the organization, but is driven by who its leader is.

The roles of external agencies and organizations are another important facet of how community leadership shapes education in rural areas. In many cases, professional assistance and support in rural communities is delivered through university partnerships and extension offices that are headquartered in cities far outside the community. This means that visiting "experts" live in urban areas hours and hundreds of miles away. Their disconnection and distance from the community often leads to misdiagnosis and subsequently poor design and bad implementation. Yet the cycle perpetuates, partly because the outside experts visit only during the diagnosis and implementation phases, and don't stick around to see the intervention fall apart or fail. Another reason outsiders are given preference is that politicians and funders believe there isn't capacity locally to administer funds and reports. Nearly always, funding is diverted to pay the salaries of outside experts.

The impact of outside agencies being seen as "experts" and awarded grants is particularly pronounced in rural communities that have been historically marginalized. In the book *Rebuilding Native Nations*, Manley Begay et al. discuss the difficulty of empowering community leaders in Native American/Alaska Native communities.[33] They argue that many of these communities need to be convinced that they are perfectly capable of identifying their own challenges and solutions, completely outside of the organizations that have been led (often by outsiders) to serve them. The authors note that, as Indigenous leaders try to address urgent problems, they, like other rural community leaders, face tremendous pressure from many individuals who know them personally and are counting on them to make immediate changes. Successful local leaders are those who are able to balance immediate needs with a strategic and long-term vision. They create programs that do not rely on their own presence to succeed, but rather build a pipeline of local talent and develop appropriate collaborations with support agencies and organizations.

FORCES ARE EMBEDDED IN RURAL COMMUNITIES' SOCIAL, CULTURAL, AND ECONOMIC HISTORIES

The forces of population stability, economic vitality, and community leadership are deeply embedded in the social, cultural, and economic history of communities. And this history is greatly affected by the geography and settling patterns in a community.[34] One clear example of the forces at work can be found in Native American nations across the United States. Overall, the Indigenous people of North America have experienced a history of genocide, forced relocations, cultural extermination, and discrimination.

These atrocities significantly impact population stability, economic vitality, and community leadership, and therefore education. For example, forced relocations of Native Americans in the 1800s continue to affect how rural Native Nations and their schools function. Consider the long-term effects of the Trail of Tears, a forced relocation in the mid-1800s of more than sixty thousand Native Americans, mostly Cherokees, Choctaws, and Creeks, from the southeastern United States to land west of the Mississippi in what is now Oklahoma. In the 1860s, the Navajo were also forced on the Long Walk to leave their homelands en masse. Anthropologists point out how the collective trauma of these forced relocations is carried through generations and continues to shape the identity of Native Americans.[35]

There is also a sad legacy of cultural extermination perpetrated on Native Americans by federal and state governments through public boarding schools. Established in the late 1800s, the boarding schools were used to forcibly assimilate Native Americans into European-American white culture. Native languages, traditional dress, and hairstyles were banned. Again, the legacy of the boarding schools continues to shape rural schooling for Native Americans. As one historian emphasizes:[36]

> Perhaps the most fundamental conclusion that emerges from boarding school histories is the profound complexity of their historical legacy for Indian people's lives ... These institutions, intended to assimilate Native people into mainstream society and eradicate Native cultures, became integral components of American Indian identities and eventually fueled the drive for political and cultural self-determination.

The history of Native American rural communities is one of the clearer examples of how population stability, economic vitality, and community leadership are embedded in particular contexts. The legacy of slavery and sharecropping in the South, migrant farm labor in the West, and coal mining in Central Appalachia are other instances where the history of a community plays a huge role in how these forces shape education.

In this chapter we've presented three forces—population stability, economic vitality, and community leadership—that shape education in rural communities. We have also shown how these elements are deeply embedded in the social, cultural, and economic histories of communities. In the next four chapters, we look closely at the educational pipeline in rural areas, from early childhood through college and career readiness. In each chapter, we highlight key tensions facing rural schools at each stage. We then illustrate, through case studies, how these forces shape educational efforts in various contexts and applications. In doing so, we show how and why these forces matter.

PART II

Meeting the Needs of Rural Students

4

Early Childhood
Education and Care

NO MATTER WHAT LENS you take to education, everyone can find common ground in the need to serve young children. From a business and leadership perspective, early education represents an incredible investment.[1] From an intervention perspective, high-quality early education centers have made meaningful, long-term differences in the lives of people who grew up in poverty, making it more likely they will be married, have a stable job, and stay out of the criminal justice system.[2] And, from a college and career readiness perspective, we understand that gaps children bring with them to kindergarten are hard to overcome as schooling progresses.[3] Plus, as we will discuss here, when we work with young children, we open up a gateway to partner with families and provide connections and supports that can be transformative, particularly in tightly networked rural communities.

Of course, there are no easy solutions, particularly in small communities that are already stressed and have maxed out small budgets for services. But we also want to embrace the hopefulness of high-quality early education and care settings, as these have been shown, over and again, to be some of the most promising, meaningful, and lasting ways to support children and families. Not only that, the best early childhood programs integrate the needs of a community with the education of a child, and are therefore positioned right at the heart of the interdependence that is a key strength of rural communities. We have seen rural early education and care settings execute on this promise, and we will share the stories of places that have created jobs and leadership pipelines for women, promoted important literacy skills by taking a place-based approach, and even helped mothers overcoming addiction. We have a lot to talk about in this chapter.

ECONOMIC VITALITY AND
THE ROOT OF ACHIEVEMENT GAPS

Take a moment to stop and think about a young child you know—it could be an infant, toddler, or preschooler—who is from a family that is down on their luck. Maybe it is a young single mother who doesn't have a reliable car and is struggling with isolation and depression. Maybe it is an older individual on a fixed income who was suddenly left in charge of the grandbabies, including a rambunctious two-year-old. There is a lot of research to confirm what is already intuitive for most educators—families that are really poor for many years have a hard time giving their young children the early experiences they need to succeed in school. We can picture families like the ones just described and imagine how hard it would be for that exhausted grandparent to read books to a toddler every night; indeed, that child may not even have a bed, but instead falls asleep on a couch in front of the family TV. And how would that single mother take her small child on outings, or to the library? Very depressed mothers sometimes have a hard time even making eye contact with their infants, or responding to their cries. Social isolation from lack of transportation and the stress of paying bills do not help. The more difficulties the family faces—inadequate housing, health troubles, mental health, addiction, unexpected deaths or loss of property due to natural disasters—the harder it becomes for the child to develop important learning and socioemotional skills. And while children can be very resilient to these kinds of setbacks, particularly if they are temporary, the rural children we really worry about are the ones born into a home with numerous different risk factors where the difficulties do not abate over time.[4] This entire constellation of risk factors is connected to the economic vitality of a community.

Through a series of studies that have followed children from a young age into schooling, we have learned quite a lot about why the economic difficulties of a community tend to show up in kindergarten readiness scores and to shadow children through their schooling.[5] Often, our knowledge of these developmental processes is limited to research on urban populations. However, the Family Life Project is a multidisciplinary research project that was intentionally designed to provide a deeper understanding of the challenges faced by young rural children and their families, as well as the strengths they bring to bear.[6] This study was created by researchers at both the University of North Carolina and Penn State; it started with 1,292 children who are representative of every baby born in 2003–2004 in six rural counties in Pennsylvania and North Carolina. These same children have been followed since then to help us understand how aspects of their lives influence their development. This research helps us focus on skills that develop from birth and prepare a rural child for success in school, no matter how easy or difficult their life.

In general, this program of research has found that children who receive warm and responsive attention—from mothers, grandparents, and fathers—develop an array of language and socioemotional skills that help them navigate obstacles. These findings are consistent with what we know about child development in any type of community, whether it is rural or urban, wealthy or poor. However, in addition to these findings, the study has also shown how community factors can create (or hinder) stability for families and outcomes for children. For example, they found that some parents had erratic work hours, and that this irregularity was particularly stressful for the entire family. We can understand how our three factors—economic vitality, population stability, and leadership—can create these conditions. For example, we know a young mother who works at a Family Dollar store. When the nearby coal mine laid off fifty workers, her job was also affected. She had once been reliably scheduled for twenty hours per week, but after the layoff her manager was sending her home early and her hours dwindled to around eight, making her childcare situation incredibly difficult. This type of instability has been documented in Latino families, and immigrants and migrants are particularly vulnerable.[7]

OPIOIDS AND YOUNG CHILDREN

One day, when Sky picked up our youngest son from preschool, he seemed unusually upset, announcing that he didn't want to talk about his day. A little concerned, she buckled him into his car seat so they could go and get his older brother. By the time they reached the elementary school, three-year-old Perry was in tears. "What is wrong?" Sky asked. "Sometimes mommies make bad decisions and they have to go to jail," Perry managed to get out. "I don't want *my* mommy to go to jail." And with that, he broke down in a full sob, convinced that at any moment his mommy and daddy would end up far away from him in the dreaded land of jail, while he and his brother would have to fend for themselves all alone.

Some of you will instantly know why a three-year-old was suddenly afraid of his mommy going to jail. The mother of one of his little friends had made a bad decision—around drugs, of course—and had been arrested. The preschool teachers at his center had spent the day building literacy and numeracy, trying to promote problem solving and using words instead of fists. They had zipped up pants and doled out meals and made sure small children washed their hands and used tissues and hung up their coats. And they also had to help a child process the loss of his mother during a time when opioids are epidemic in many of our rural communities, and a growing problem among women who are pregnant and have small children. There are very real and serious issues lurking around early childhood, and we want to take a holistic look at how we can provide services that offer a life raft for families who are on an ocean of chaos and uncertainty.

Increasingly, expectant and new mothers are a focus of addiction treatment in rural America. Rural women are one of the fastest-growing demographics in the opioid epidemic. One example of a community leader making a difference for small families is Tim Robinson of Addiction Recovery Care in Louisa, Kentucky. The program has recently opened Karen's Place, a home for pregnant and new mothers who are getting treatment for addiction. The center allows the mothers and young babies to live together for treatment for as long as needed in the pregnancy and for up to three months after delivery. This is the type of focused service delivery model that can change lives and families.

Again, a strength of our rural communities is the ability to identify individuals who are most at need and coordinate services for them, both within and beyond school walls. For example, a rural community can help mothers who are grappling with addiction. See the sidebar for a further discussion of opioids and young children. We would be remiss if we did not point out the potential for partnerships with medical care providers. Whether or not a family participates in any early childhood programming, they will most likely need to access medical care. Deborah Erwin, a surgeon and researcher at the University of Arkansas, spent a great deal of time with Latino families that had immigrated to rural Arkansas to better understand how they integrated into their communities and accessed medical care.[8] One of her findings was that maternity care was a touchpoint for immigrant families—they all accessed care, no matter what cultural or language barriers were in place. Maternity care, then, is one potential area to catch families that might not otherwise receive any formalized supports until their children are in kindergarten. In some states, well-child visits become a time to screen for language development and make referrals for early intervention.[9]

Of course, one of the very best ways we can support families is through a strong system of early education and care settings that provide high-quality learning experiences from birth through age five.[10] Early childhood education has a long history in rural America. In 1964, President Johnson chose Appalachian Kentucky, where he crouched with the Fletcher family on their porch in Martin County, as the place to gain support for his War on Poverty.[11] The sweeping legislation that followed established the federal Head Start programs, which had a specific focus on both urban and rural communities. Ever since, early childhood programs have been seen as a major tool in promoting equal opportunities for rural communities. But rural communities face two large challenges in providing early education and care: the first is access, and the second is quality. We next look at each one of these challenges and learn how they can potentially be combated at the local, state, and federal level.

THE NEED FOR EARLY EDUCATION AND CARE IN RURAL AMERICA

Although families are the foundation of children's development, high-quality early care and education have the potential to be life-changing, particularly in communities facing economic challenges.[12]

High-quality early childhood programs have been shown to boost cognitive functioning and reduce special education placements.[13] But that is just the beginning of the benefits they offer. Quality care centers improve health outcomes and are particularly helpful in identifying children who need early intervention to support their development. The effects of good programming extend beyond the child, facilitating good outcomes for the parents as well. Mothers of children in excellent early care settings are healthier, more likely to work, and are better able to continue their own education. Economists project that every dollar spent on early care programming for children three to four years old results in a 7 to 10 percent return on investment, with a potential of a 14 percent ROI for top-notch, wraparound services from birth to age five.[14]

Access to Early Education and Care

There is no question that early childhood education and care is less accessible in rural America than it is in urban or suburban communities. Fifty-nine percent of rural communities are what can be considered a "childcare desert," meaning that there are at least three children for every one slot available—if there are any options available at all.[15] Head Start is one of the few options for preschool in many rural communities; see the sidebar for more information on the outsized role that Head Start plays in rural communities. However, even with programs like Early Head Start, shortages are worse if you focus on infants and toddlers. For example, in rural Oregon, there is childcare capacity for only 14.7 percent of the infant-toddler population. Not surprisingly, the shortages are the greatest in low-income rural communities. The group with the least access to childcare is composed of rural Native Americans and Alaska Natives living in poverty, with Latino families close behind.

There are many reasons why providing access to childcare is more difficult in rural communities, but to be clear, the shortage is not from lack of demand. Although some stereotypes of rural

America may imply that fewer people there work outside the home, the reality is that there are many working parents in rural America. About 60 percent of mothers of children under five in rural census tracts work outside of the home, which is roughly equivalent to mothers in urban settings. The Family Life Project (FLP) looked carefully at the hours worked by the mothers in its study, and the findings were similar. Interestingly, they drilled down on the number of hours women worked based on whether they were considered very poor, near poor, or not poor. They found that even the mothers in their study who were considered "very poor" worked a similar number of hours to those in other groups—an average of twenty-two hours per week.[16]

THE ROLE OF HEAD START IN RURAL COMMUNITIES

There is no doubt that Head Start plays an outsized role in providing center-based care in rural communities. One in three rural children who go to preschool attend a Head Start program. In "Frontier" communities—a designation by the US Census Bureau given to communities with sparse population density that are more than an hour from a town of fifty thousand or more—nearly half of all early education centers are Head Start programs. Head Start is an important way to bring federal funding to communities that do not have sufficient numbers of children to create a market for early education and care. In the West, where a great percentage of land is untaxable because it is controlled by the Bureau of Land Management or is part of a Native nation, federally funded programs are particularly important.

Anyone who has done the calculations on how to afford childcare is probably familiar with the conundrum faced by the rural mothers in the FLP study. If you work twenty-two hours per week at minimum wage (currently $7.25 an hour unless a specific state sets a different rate), that amounts to $160 per week and an annual pay of $8,294. Where is the money to pay for childcare? Again, one finding from the FLP is that irregular work hours for the mother is particularly stressful on families. Most childcare arrangements are not set up to accommodate fluctuations in days and time, particularly when work hours sometimes extend well beyond nine to five. This means that poor families must rely on family and friends to provide care and are not able to use the licensed centers that are far more likely to focus on learning experiences.

Given this potential set of circumstances, it is not surprising that rural parents who need childcare are more likely to use home-based than center-based care. Home providers are often cheaper and more flexible. Interestingly, the FLP found that very poor mothers were the least likely to use state-sponsored childcare options. Instead, not-poor mothers were most likely to enroll their children in state-funded preschool, while very poor mothers continued to rely on home-based care. The differences in the type of setting bring us to the second important facet of early education and care for young children—quality. You may not be surprised to hear that the home-based settings were also rated lower in quality by researchers who evaluated settings using standardized tools for quality.

Quality Early Care

Across all settings, achieving high-quality early education and care at scale is a vexing problem. After all, the benefits associated with using early education and care are all intimately linked to the quality of the setting.[17] Otherwise, in general, early education and care settings tend to just replicate the quality of interactions that are already happening at the home. The families that we described earlier in the chapter who struggle to connect with their children and build their knowledge through language primarily access care settings with the exact same challenges. Families with more disposable income and less stress not only can afford trips and educational excursions, but they also send their children to better early care settings that promote learning.

At a state level, policy makers and economists have thought of ways to increase the quality of the settings available to children from poor families. For example, Minneapolis Federal Reserve economists Art Rolnick and Rob Grunewald have been champions of early education and care as a way to combat social problems.[18] They sought to create a thriving marketplace of superior early care options while simultaneously administering scholarships to families who would otherwise struggle to afford this level of care. To participate and receive the dollars, the childcare setting had to go through a quality-rating process. Of course, it can be hard to imagine how a program like this would work in a more rural area where there are fewer childcare options. Thankfully, we have an example of just how this particular approach was implemented in rural Grand Rapids, Minnesota, a lumber mill town of around ten thousand about 175 miles north of Minneapolis in north central Minnesota.[19]

As it happens, the town of Grand Rapids has a tremendous asset that many rural communities do not, and that is a charitable foundation that competitively administers grants for projects that improve the town and the larger region of Itasca County. This organization, the Blandin Foundation, was set up by a wealthy family that owned a paper mill in the town. On the heels of Rolnick and Grunewald's work in the Twin Cities area, a group of local leaders approached the Blandin Foundation board in March 2004 with a proposal to create high-quality early childcare in their community, following the lead of the Twin Cities. One of these leaders, Mary Kosak, said: "We set the stage and let the Blandin Foundation know that this wasn't going to be cheap. It was a good thing we set the stage, too. It had to be a commitment by the Foundation—it couldn't be a one- or even two-year grant. It had to be a minimum of a ten-year commitment."

Over the next several months the committee developed an in-depth proposal that focused on four components: quality, intensity, accountability, and a system that worked for children and families. Multiple meetings were held to garner support from the community and nationally recognized experts were called upon for their feedback. Indeed, they invited Rolnick and Grunewald to give input on their plan, along with experts in school change and early childhood education efforts. The result of all of this work was an organization called Invest Early.

Invest Early was more than a replication of the efforts in Minneapolis. In the end, the committed group of local leaders who started Invest Early realized that the model would have to be changed to work in Grand Rapids. As Kosak explains: "In places like Itasca County, Art Rolnick's model of scholarships is difficult to implement. We chose to depart from Rolnick and Grunewald's model and instead of giving scholarships to parents, we granted funds directly to educational providers." What they did instead was to enroll families in Invest Early for free through a simple application process, helping them identify the center that made the most sense and granting the money for their spot directly to the setting. Then, on the back end, they worked hard to raise the quality of all early education and care settings in their community.

How did they do this? How do you take a disparate group of private day care centers, Head Start programs, and home-based care settings and increase the quality across the board? In particular, the organization focused on the human capital in their community and on creating a ladder of career opportunities in education. This began by coordinating trainings across the many different types of settings, and then working with the local community college to help the childcare workers access increased training and qualifications in education. This tackles one of the pernicious issues in early education and care, namely that the median wage in a childcare center is still at the poverty level. But by creating a career pipeline, working in an early care center was one step toward a higher-paying job in education, moving women from family-care settings to center-based settings, and some into teaching positions in K–12 schools.

Invest Early is a beautiful example of how a rural community created a strategic initiative to improve the early learning experiences of its small children. The organization made childcare more affordable for families living in poverty while also working to increase the quality of teachers and programming. Because they worked with a variety of types of centers, they helped promote quality not only in preschool, but also in settings that serve infants and toddlers. Even more, they created family stability through an educational and career pipeline that, in the end, helped mothers the most. Strong local leadership overcame barriers presented by economic and social conditions.

Mississippi First is an educational advocacy and policy group that is doing work similar to Invest Early, but its focus is on state-level change. One of the keystones of its work is establishing Early Learning Collaboratives, including passing the Early Learning Collaborative Act. Early Learning Collaboratives provide an avenue for the state to fund programs for three- and four-year-old children across the state. But rather than focusing only on prekindergarten programs in the public school system, the collaboratives are set up to promote coordination across a variety of settings. Again, by improving private day care centers and Head Start, they are helping increase quality in the many settings used by rural families in need of care.

The Early Learning Collaborative Act set aside funding that brings dollars to communities that establish a collaborative and then apply for grants. The focus of the collaboratives, not surprisingly, is on connecting community stakeholders in a variety of early education and care settings. In fact, to establish a collaborative, a community must at minimum bring together leadership from both a Head Start program and a school district, although they are encouraged to include private day care centers and parochial options. One of the hallmarks of the Early Learning Collaboratives is their emphasis on quality and accountability. Collaborative preK programs are required to meet the highest standards, as defined by meeting ten of ten benchmarks set by the National Institute for Early Education Research (NIEER).[20] All participants in a collaborative must administer the preK version of the kindergarten-readiness assessment in the fall and spring of the preK year so that the public can assess how much each program is growing its students, regardless of their starting point. The results for Mississippi have been positive. Children who participate in Early Learning Collaboratives score higher on kindergarten readiness measures than the average child in Mississippi.

EARLY EDUCATION AND CARE EMBEDDED
IN FAMILIES AND COMMUNITIES

Invest Early and Mississippi First are both great examples of systemic change. But if you are a teacher or leader in one community, they may be beyond your reach in your current role. Little School is an example of one smaller program that was flexible enough to meet the needs of a specific community, and was implemented quickly with a limited budget. Little School is an early childhood program that we developed at Pine Mountain Settlement School, an educational nonprofit in Harlan County, Kentucky. This part of the Appalachian Mountains is undeniably rural—we have to drive eleven miles to the closest post office, and even that one is considered a rural outpost that is open only two hours a day, five days per week. When we moved there, we had a five-year-old and a five-month-old, and the closest center that offered infant care was over an hour's drive away, one way, and in the opposite direction of our work. Years of economic decline and population loss meant that few families around us had two adults in the workforce. In short, there was very limited demand for traditional childcare that would provide a place for families to drop off young children during business hours. An elementary school about twenty minutes away offered half-day prekindergarten programming for four-year-olds, but we found that all other services involved an early educator visiting a small number of children. One popular model was to develop a bus that would drive to the home so that the child and a caretaker could then sit together on the bus and learn kindergarten readiness skills. But there was certainly still reason to think that children too young for kindergarten would benefit from a program that brought families together to offer learning and social opportunities. In fact, early learning was one of the biggest requests we heard from community members, again and again.

Given the clear need and demand, we decided to create our own program that was responsive to our specific location. The goal from the outset was to promote language development, early learning skills, and social and emotional skills in young children. But that was just the start, because we were looking to create a program that was for the whole family. In particular, we sought to combat social isolation and give caretakers a setting where they could feel connected and supported by others who were raising young children. This goal reflected the changing needs due to population change, as families and friends had increasingly moved away in order to make a living. There were few families looking for childcare coverage for work, and so including the adults made good sense as a way to strengthen the whole family.

For practical reasons, we opened it up to children of all ages. It was clear that if we targeted a specific age range—say, three-year-olds—that we would not have enough children. The youngest participant we ever had was a couple of weeks old, and occasionally older children would join. Most children, however, were two or three years old. The program operated for two hours a day, three days per week, and was intentionally set up in partnership with the closest preK program—a bus would take the children from our community directly to Little School after their program ended to add two hours to their day (plus an extra meal). Little School was a gathering time for everyone, a chance to come together informally, socialize, and learn.

The day was a combination of structured and unstructured activities and included a free nutritious lunch for adults and children alike that often featured food grown right on campus on the five-acre organic farm that was part of the education center. Between grants, donations, and items from our own home, we set up a classroom with plenty of flexible learning centers for exploration that were age-appropriate for children from tiny babies to kindergartners. Families arrived during a time for centers-based exploration, allowing them a flexible entry and a chance to get settled. A teacher (Sky) and an assistant (our community coordinator and grandmother of two of the children) rotated among the children with the specific goal of building language. The caregivers were freed from their usual duties with their children, and instead gathered and chatted together. Yet, they were in the same room, so they were always witness to the ways that the teachers talked with their children. After about thirty minutes of open-ended play there was a story time, song, and bathroom time. Children then lined up for lunch, where the group sang a song of prayer before eating. After lunch, there was almost always time for some type of outdoor exploration or play, and if the weather was too bad, we found inside ways to move our bodies and get a little exercise.

The curriculum built on the strengths of the local community. It was place-based and closely tied to the natural environment. We visited the farm and had all manner of seasonal centers. When we played with clay, we also made seed balls from heritage bean seeds that could be planted in the children's gardens—they all had a garden at home. When spring came, we went and hunted for morel mushrooms, called "hickory chickens" locally. But we were also constantly stretching the experiences and the conversations. For example, we became a partner with the PBS Ready to Learn grant for rural communities and hosted family workshops on software coding and STEM.

Did Little School have any impact on the children? That would be almost impossible to say in an educational climate that values data and testing. If you have a regular group of fifteen children, some infants, some toddlers, and some preschoolers, there are very few measures that can capture growth. Instead, we had our collection of moments and stories—what would be called participant action research—that gave us information on the needs of our children and the impacts on their lives.[21] We witnessed children read their first words, and a few cases where they held books or art supplies for the first time. But even more, we saw changes in families over time. One mother came in the week after her partner had died in a car accident, completely stricken. She was soothed by the women who gathered while her three children had a chance to play, relax, and eat. She stayed with us for several months until her life was settled again, and she found a job. We found beds for families that had none for their children and took in a little girl whose mother was imprisoned due to her addiction. When the mother got clean, Geoff hired her to work in the cafeteria, where she has been employed and clean ever since. After we had operated about a year, a mother confided one day that she had left a domestic violence situation because of Little School. Her husband had refused to let her go anywhere with family or friends, but he let her bring the children to Little School. It was there, talking with the other mothers and grandmothers, that she realized her situation was not normal or acceptable. And it was over months in this setting that she built up the courage to leave. Her first job in her new life was with Pine Mountain Settlement School.

Little School shows us that not all early childhood efforts have to be formalized, drop-off care settings. In fact, Sky moved on to become a state extension specialist, and one thing she did in her new role was to create curricular materials in an effort to scale up the experience of Little School through extension. The curricular materials included hands-on and place-based activities that could be led by extensions agents or volunteers at farmer's markets and summer feeding programs, with caregivers nearby. We have many opportunities to bring families together for learning, and they can be simple and inexpensive.

RURAL EARLY CHILDHOOD SERVICES AT WORK

Ultimately, what our young rural children need are champions who are willing to assess needs and create a response that fits with the tools at hand. Mississippi First, Invest Early, and Little School all operate at very different levels, from the hyperlocal to the state level. One is in Appalachia, another in the Midwest, and still another in the Deep South. And yet they all share some commonalities that speak to the forces at work in rural communities. They create affordable options for families living in poverty. They involve community leaders to make connections across a variety of programs and services.

With vast distances and irregular employment patterns, there is no one neat and tidy system that can capture all children who need care from nine to five while parents are at work. Yes, universal and free preK through the public school system is a very important part of that effort. And Head Start plays an undeniably central role in providing access to care in rural America. But we need greater coordination from birth all the way to age five if we are to fully support families. If we are to do it right, we must partner with local doctor's offices, family care providers, and postsecondary training programs along with the early childhood providers. There are plenty of entry points, both large and small, for any teacher or school leader. After all, the call for high-quality early education and care is clear and compelling, and right now there are hundreds of thousands of infants and toddlers in rural America who are counting on us to provide them with a lifetime of opportunity. We turn next to the needs of children and families as children begin school and learn to read.

5

Literacy for Rural Children

IN UNDERSTANDING READING DEVELOPMENT, researchers and practitioners have often focused on the universal: the letters and sounds that need to come together in first grade and kindergarten, the passages and vocabulary lists of the middle grades, and the textbooks and writing assignments of high school. But the field of literacy also has a strong tradition of seeking out the nuances and particularities of specific communities of children as a way to create a more personal and relevant experience. Nowhere is this tradition truer than for rural communities. In 1963, Sylvia Ashton-Warner published *Teacher*, a compelling read on how she made reading emotional and relevant for her rural Maori students in New Zealand by starting with the words of their dreams and nightmares, beginning literacy instructions with words like *skeleton*.[1] The first book of the Foxfire series, a collection of oral histories and folk instructions compiled by Eliot Wigginton's students in North Georgia, appeared in 1972.[2] These colorful books inspired a new approach to student-centered and place-based learning. And this is just the beginning of a list of passionate rural educators, like Teresa McCarty, who told the story of how Rough Rock Demonstration School in Arizona gave students a "place to be Navajo."[3]

In this chapter we will take that passion, those deep connections to place and people that are the strengths of rural communities, and link them to the larger evidence base of what makes for strong literacy instruction. We want to articulate a clearer understanding of literacy development for culturally and linguistically diverse students living in rural communities. We'll take a close look at one of the most dynamic groups of rural students, English language learners. The premise of this chapter is that reading difficulties are not a given for rural students, no matter what challenges they may face. Instead, we look across reading development for an understanding of the conditions that nurture good outcomes for rural students. And, of course, we look at these in relation to our three forces: economic vitality, population stability, and community leadership.

LEARNING TO READ

From preschool through third grade, we often think of learning to read as the key challenge for students. Children begin to understand that the symbols they see on a page represent letters, and that these letters represent sounds and words. In kindergarten, the work is breaking these words and sounds apart. Over time, children become faster and more facile with letters, sounds, and words they know by heart (i.e., sight words). The mapping becomes less about the actual letters and words and more about the meanings they hold. Written words then flow together to tell stories and give information, just like spoken language.

Where the breakdown occurs for most children has little to do with the early word-reading stage. Although some children initially struggle to sound out the words on the page, most eventually establish the procedural skills of reading, such as decoding and letter naming. We even have some good evidence that this is particularly true in rural communities. When Sky investigated the early literacy skills of kindergartners in Appalachian Kentucky, she found that by the end of the year, the students were above the national average in phonics skills, with median scores that mapped closest to the beginning of second grade. Similarly, the Family Life Project, which is closely following the language and literacy development of over a thousand rural, low-income students in North Carolina and Pennsylvania, reported scores near the national norm in letter naming and recognition in first grade.[4] The problem is that the gaps in students' oral language skills—typically measured by analyzing a child's vocabulary—can continue to lag even once a child has mastered the fundamentals of phonics.[5] Moreover, entry-level differences of these meaning-based proficiencies appear to be compounded over time; for example, vocabulary levels become more discrepant during the primary grades.[6] Research shows that economic conditions are deeply tied to reading as a developmental process. This issue can be particularly difficult for English language learners, as described in more detail in the sidebar.

LEARNING TO READ FOR ENGLISH LANGUAGE LEARNERS

Although we often take it for granted that ELLs will encounter more reading difficulties, this is not necessarily the case for decoding skills. The process of matching symbols to sounds is fundamentally the same across different languages. In fact, with some early literacy skills, like phonological awareness, ELLs may have an advantage because their experience with multiple languages better trains them to hear the individual sounds in words. Moreover, instruction in alphabet knowledge and letter sounds translates easily from one language to another. Thus a kindergartner who arrives from another country won't necessarily face major interruptions in their knowledge. For these students especially we need to understand that "reading" means much more than deciphering words on a page.

Like so many other rural students, ELLs will master the sound-symbol correspondences and thus be able to "read" the words on the page, but they have underdeveloped vocabulary to make meaning of what they are reading. Ultimately, limited early learning experiences and opportunities with books will impact comprehension scores far more than decoding. Despite appearing to be strong "early readers," over time, ELLs' compromised meaning-making impedes their academic achievement. At the same time, irrespective of the assessments in place, educators are much more likely to take a "wait and see" approach with these students—assuming that with more years of schooling, they will overcome their weaknesses in the domain of reading. However, ample data on the performance of ELL students suggests that without more tailored, intense instructional supports, this population doesn't just "catch up." A heavy focus on phonics is even more detrimental to our ELLs.

Although all reading skills are required, in coordination, for proficient reading, language is far more likely to pose long-standing difficulties as it is a central part of comprehension. Within "language" is a vast universe of words, languages, structures, and knowledge that is far more complex than the twenty-six letters and forty-four sounds in the English language that we use to decode. Ultimately, it is our language abilities that are associated with long-term reading achievement.[7] And while the rural kindergartners and first graders we just mentioned had a strong foundation in phonological skills, they lagged behind national norms in measures of language. As educators on the Navajo Nation, a setting where children faced these challenges with the additional obstacle of learning the English language, we could see that the struggles rural students encounter are even greater for ELLs.

THE RELATIONSHIP OF LANGUAGE TO READING

The connections between culture, socioeconomic status, and long-term reading achievement are complex, particularly in the realm of language. Have you ever heard of the thirty million word gap? The idea behind it is that children living in poverty can enter school having heard thirty million fewer words than their classmates from professional families. This potentially plays a big role in achievement gaps, since vocabulary is one of the most important elements of reading comprehension after third grade, when children need to read to learn. The idea of a thirty million word gap came from Hart and Risley's book *Meaningful Differences in the Everyday Experience of Young American Children*, originally published in 1995.[8] These two researchers undertook an innovative and very laborious research study. Through careful analysis of periodic recordings of mother and child conversations from age ten months to three years, the authors were able to quantify aspects of the early language environment. The sample of 42 "well-functioning" families included 13 children whose parents were professionals, 23 children whose parents held blue-collar jobs, and 6 children whose families subsisted on welfare. The major findings of the study were large—actually, staggering—differences among the three groups in the sheer number of words the children heard. They calculated that if you added up every difference in the number of words heard between the three groups that it would result in a thirty-million-word deficit by age four for children who grew up in poverty.

This study has since come under fire for a number of reasons, including extrapolating beyond the data at hand and suggesting that the only conversational partner for a small child is the mother.[9] At the same time, this is just one of many studies that has found real differences in the language experiences of a child based on the environment in which they grow up—exactly the same kinds of issues as the three forces of economic vitality, population stability, and community leadership that we discuss in this book. These differences are worth paying attention to because they are very closely connected to a child's language skills at school entry, and those skills are a strong predictor of how well a child will learn to read and their overall academic achievement.[10] For example, the Home-School Study of Language and Literacy Development (HSSLD) followed children from age three all the way through high school. Would you believe that tenth-grade reading achievement could be predicted from the language a child heard at home at three years old?[11]

Today we have a more nuanced understanding of how language impacts reading ability than we did in 1995. We now know, for example, that you do not need a talkative caretaker to succeed in school. The bigger difference maker is not the number of words a child hears, but rather the variety and complexity of language the mother (or other caretaker) uses in talking with the child. In fact, in the HSSLD, 50 percent of the differences found in a second-grade vocabulary test could be traced back to the complexity and variety of words the child heard from their mother as a five-year-old, even though the children in this study all lived in poverty and were all from a similar geographic background. These findings were also true for the rural children in the Family Life Project—it was the complexity of the language a child heard that predicted their language skills at three years, not the simple quantity.

What we need to be careful of is assuming that our children somehow have deficient language backgrounds. We need to be even more cautious when making judgments about the abilities of our students who are learning English language, as we discuss in the sidebar. Navigating the stereotype of poor language skills is especially crucial for rural areas. How often have we heard the stereotype of the quiet rural person? In movies and popular media, silent and staring children and adults become the backdrop of the terrifying and menacing rural community, as in *Deliverance* and *Children of the Corn*. The silent Native American is another token figure. And the butt of a common joke is the country dweller who doesn't have the language skills to give adequate directions, instructing the visitor from out of town to "turn right by where the Jenkins' barn burned down."

Lessons Learned from Eastern Washington State

Linda Smith is the principal of a Title I elementary school in Eastern Washington where half of the students are Hispanic. In her thirty years in education, Smith has witnessed many changes as small, family-owned cherry and apple orchards have increasingly been bought out for large-scale agribusiness. In that time, the school population has gone from mostly white to an increasing number of immigrant and migrant students. Now, Smith says, large-scale businesses rely on companies that bring in seasonal workers through guest work visas that do not allow children to follow along. There are still a few students in school seasonally, but far fewer than in past years. That said, the school still serves a high number of children of immigrants, many of whom come from households in which all adults work full time. At home the only language is Spanish, and many children come to school with almost no English language skills. Smith's experience emphasizes what is known in the literature: these are smart and hard-working students, and the transition from Spanish to English may take time but does not hold her students back. Smith cautions educators that when reading difficulties arise with immigrant students, they require extra support and remediation, just like some peers who speak only English.[12] "It's very important to hold students to high learning standards for reading, even when they are learning English," she says. Most of all, she expresses her admiration for these hard-working families who are making a new life in the fruit industry.

Those who are from, or deeply embedded in, rural communities know a different truth. We have yet to spend time in a rural community where we did not find incredibly rich language traditions, especially around humor. Rural folks can get you laughing. And boy, can they preach and pray. Even researchers who study sociolinguistics know that children from low-income communities become excellent speakers, using a·style that is both complex and creative.[13] But caregiver talkativeness alone does not predict vocabulary or language skills.[14]

When we look closely at a community, we can get a window into how language socialization practices shape literacy outcomes for children. The foundational work in this field is Shirley Brice Heath's ethnography of small-town communities in the Carolina Piedmont.[15] Heath spent decades documenting the language experiences of children within their home communities and how these intersected with the expectations and practices of school. Indeed, reading difficulties seemed nearly inevitable for the children from the predominantly African American working-class neighborhood of Trackton; as much affection and love as these children received from their families and neighbors, and as lyrical as their spoken speech, school represented a universe apart from home. Once they entered first grade, these children were suddenly expected to sit and complete worksheets, to answer questions unlike any they had ever been asked, and to understand stories about unfamiliar topics in a completely different narrative style than what they were used to. As a result, the children of Trackton often struggled in school, both behaviorally and academically, and particularly when compared to their classmates whose home lives mapped more closely to the language and behavioral expectations of school. Accordingly, they brought home report cards with lower grades, were more often in trouble, and did not make it to high school graduation as often as peers whose parents held professional jobs. The children from Roadville, the white working-class community, also struggled, although with different aspects of the school environment. In particular, these children often hit roadblocks around fourth grade, when asked to answer inferential questions and analyze more complex texts. The difficulties were even more pronounced when school leaders were unfamiliar with the lives of their students and could not use instruction to help bridge to new ways of using language.

The Trackton of *Ways with Words* is its own unique context specific to a particular historical period in the United States; however, it is not the only low-income community with poor academic outcomes, where home styles of language did not map well onto school expectations.[16] Indeed, it has been argued that a mismatch between home and school settings may be a primary cause of reading difficulties, and that children need explicit instruction for navigating the language of school as much as they need instruction in letter-naming skills.[17] Findings from a variety of studies suggest a misalignment between the type of knowledge privileged by schools and the early experiences of children in historically marginalized communities.[18]

Such conflicting findings point to the different types of language skill necessary for proficiency in the home and school environments, including the more conceptually abstract "academic language" knowledge that school contexts demand.[19] Thus, a major challenge in promoting educational equality for children from disadvantaged backgrounds is identifying pathways for their verbal expertise—the "funds of knowledge" they bring with them to school—to serve as assets in developing the wide repertoire of linguistic skills called upon in academic discourse.[20] This kind of work calls on strong instructional leadership, especially when navigating quickly shifting rural populations, or places where financial resources strain families and communities.

ACCESS TO PRINT

Most children come to school having observed members of their community using print in their everyday lives, but there are still systematic differences in the amount and quality of exposure to print in general and books specifically.[21] For example, in Heath's ethnography, she found a variety of literacies in everyday life, such as using print to read labels on cans, compare prices, memorize Bible passages, and write lists and greeting cards. Certain everyday occasions called for more complex use of print: leading a prayer at church meant scripting out points to cover; dress patterns and car repair guides were pored over in order to follow directions carefully. However, in these same communities, many children did not see parents reading books for pleasure and were not likely to get a bedtime story.

Shared book reading is an unusually beneficial experience for language development; it is associated with vocabulary gains because it provides a particularly word-rich experience for children, and mothers are more likely to use the type of unfamiliar and sophisticated words that build vocabulary when reading books compared with other activities.[22] A number of interventions that have successfully boosted language outcomes in three- to five-year-olds living in poverty have involved training parents in reading interactively with children.[23] Some argue that print is the best route to equalizing educational outcomes.[24] And let us not forget that books are one of the best ways to quickly deepen knowledge. Even the simplest of picture books contain happenings far beyond what we have lived, seen, or experienced. While helping our students learn to read, we need to embrace good and rich texts.

We know that in general, children from low-income urban communities have a harder time finding books, and are less likely to have books read to them based on proximity alone.[25] If distance can create barriers in urban communities, we can easily imagine how this could be magnified in very rural communities. The Pew Charitable Trust reports that more than one in five nonmetro people live more than six miles from a library, and we would guess that the distance range is large.[26] Even within Appalachian Kentucky, we have moved from one rural location that required us to travel forty-five minutes one way to a library, to a different town that has two libraries with a children's section, both of which are minutes away.

Community leaders can make a big difference in how easily a parent can pick up a book to read to a young child. Dolly Parton, for example, took a leadership role to make it easy for young children in East Tennessee to get books mailed directly to their door every month of their life from birth until age five. Our youngest child was once enrolled in Dolly's Imagination Library (discussed further in the sidebar) and now attends a preschool that partners with Raising a Reader, a nonprofit that works to make books accessible to children living in poor communities by sending home book-bags and reading logs each week. We are dedicated bedtime book readers, but even we can recognize that this simple program makes it far easier to read higher quality books. Having a new selection of books at our fingertips every week has resulted in a far greater range of reading materials. We particularly appreciate how both of these programs have worked diligently to represent diverse lived experiences in the selection of books..

Sometimes programs that send books home, or help children read a thousand books by kindergarten, feel insufficient in the face of helping children read when we know how difficult it can be to understand textbooks or complete essays. Many teachers and administrators in rural schools worry about accountability measures.[27] Unfortunately, the kind of language skills that are built with shared book reading can be hard to measure, even if they have a much greater chance of changing ultimate reading comprehension outcomes. Taking a long view, rural community leaders are very well served to push for ways to promote reading.

THE DOLLY PARTON IMAGINATION LIBRARY

Dolly Parton, the perennially famous country singer now known for her ability to close urban-rural divides, is also a champion of rural literacy. Parton founded the Imagination Library in 1995. Her original idea was to help children from her hometown. She observed that some children start school at a disadvantage because they have had fewer books read to them. She worried that students who weren't read to as young children would feel inadequate, and they would never imagine themselves in college. The original goal of the Imagination Library was for every child in Sevier County to receive one book every month, mailed and addressed to the child, from the day they were born until the day they started kindergarten. The entire program was completely free of charge for the family and individualized to the age of the child so that siblings could each receive their own unique book. It was a simple way to break down barriers between homes and books in rural East Tennessee. What began as a hometown initiative now serves children in all fifty states, Australia, Canada, and the United Kingdom, each month mailing thousands of free books to children around the world. Our youngest child was a recipient of the Imagination Library through the Harlan County, Kentucky, public library. We were consistently impressed with the quality of the books that showed up at our door every month. Years later, several of those books are still beloved favorites that are specific requests at bedtime.

ADVANCED LITERACY SKILLS

Now that we have a better understanding of reading development for diverse children, let's think about the more advanced literacy skills that our students encounter. Academic language, which draws on the oral language skills described in this chapter, differs from the way we use language in everyday conversation. This is because one of the primary reasons for using academic language is to communicate clearly with an unknown audience who doesn't yet exist—the eventual reader of a text. In spoken language, we make use of shorter sentences and familiar words. We can clarify our meaning, offer additional information, or repeat a statement if the listener becomes confused. None of these options are possible when writing. Instead, the writing style used in informational text favors precise, explicit, and concise language. Another reason for the high prevalence of academic language in students' textbooks is that complex content is often expressed using equally complex language. Just think, for a moment, of the topics that students read about each day. In social studies, students may read about the distant past; texts in science may discuss things that we cannot see, such as gravity; and English language arts texts may demand the ability to take different perspectives in order to understand the relationships between the characters. All of these ideas would be very hard to express using simpler language.

What we're seeing in today's classrooms, especially when focusing on the needs of struggling readers, is that even students who are conversationally fluent in English may have trouble when faced with tasks that demand that they comprehend and produce academic language.[28] These students, many of whom are English language learners or speakers of a nonmainstream English dialect, find the academic language of print beyond their reach. Over time, because they can't access the words, these readers have less access to the information the texts contain. This means that they face two barriers to comprehending complex texts: low levels of both academic language and background knowledge. The result is also evident in students' writing.

EXPERIENCE, VOCABULARY, AND
ACADEMIC LANGUAGE

One year when Sky was teaching in New Mexico, the accommodation given for ELLs for the annual state test was for the test booklet and questions to be read aloud to the students. This allowed Sky to walk up and down the rows of desks, reading the passages and the questions out loud; when she paused after each question, she could see how the students filled in their bubbles, full of concentration and effort after a year of very hard work to become better readers. That year the fourth-grade test featured two informational passages on two very different topics: the first Thanksgiving, and the subway system in New York City.

You might guess whether the students in rural New Mexico had an easier time answering questions about the first Thanksgiving versus the subway system. The passage on the subway completely threw the students, whose primary knowledge of trains was the mile-long Santa Fe, stacked double-high with cargo containers but never people. The only Subway they knew was sixty miles away in town, and it was a place to buy a sandwich. For those students to wrap their heads around an underground passenger train in a city, then quickly digest information on fares and schedules, was a tremendously difficult task during a brief testing window. Predictably, those #2 pencils filled in wrong answers over and again. It was almost as if the answers were designed to trick them.

To correctly answer questions on the first Thanksgiving was an equally sophisticated task. One of the biggest challenges Sky's Navajo students faced in testing was to read a passage about different Native nations, then answer the questions. To be clear, it was not because they lacked perspective on different Native American cultures and customs. These were students who attended ceremonial gatherings that brought diverse Native communities together, and who knew well the differences between Hopi and Apache and

Navajo. The bigger problem was that almost all questions asked about the customs of "Native Americans" broadly, and the students were supposed to ignore their own reality to make a selection based on a passage. Why should they pick that "Native Americans" lived in longhouses, just because they had read a passage based on the historic lives of the Seneca people? After all, these questions almost never specified which Native Americans or when.

The reason the students were able to appropriately answer questions on the first Thanksgiving was, as luck had it, they had extensively studied the first Thanksgiving that year. They researched the true dress and actions of the Pilgrims, along with the Wampanoag. They talked about what sources of information are reliable and had reviewed picture books on the first Thanksgiving based on their accuracy. They wrote and put on a play, designing their own costumes. They even practiced answering test questions that were written as if all Native Americans were the Wampanoag of 1621. For example, they looked at a practice question that expected the reader to answer that Native Americans use wampum to purchase goods. Again, the question never specified which Native nation or time period; it just assumed that the only knowledge the reader had of Native American purchases came from the passage. The students discussed over and again that tests want the answer in the passage, even if that answer is not necessarily real or true.

The students approached this passage very differently than the one about the subway. They did not miss a beat over the name "Wampanoag" or references to colonial times. They had the background knowledge to quickly engage with the work and understood to look for the answers that were specific to the situation described, no matter how poorly stated. Even students who would be deemed "weak readers," whose Lexile levels were far below the passage, were able to take on that portion with success. You could visibly see their shoulders straighten and their jaws relax—they knew they were good.

This example highlights the key challenge facing rural students. That is, we can all be good or bad readers, depending on the text and the context in which we interact with the words. Ultimately, it is our lived experiences that have tremendous bearing on how we will interact with a text. When we want to build academic language around a text, it will take a good deal of very immersive instruction to give many students the foundation they need for success. It only makes sense that building a strong knowledge base on academic subjects is especially important for rural students. And all of us share these stories of misunderstandings, of times that the knowledge our rural students brought did not match the task at hand. One of Geoff's favorites is a passage from a practice math test that asked about stock trading. His students, who only knew about sheep and cattle, required significant instruction to learn about Wall Street and the New York Stock Exchange. But behind each one of these herculean tasks is a new world unfolding and with it a whole new range of vocabulary words.

To us, it only makes sense that making the unfamiliar at least known, if not familiar, is especially important in rural settings. Our oldest child lived his first five years in Boston, where we could hop on a subway car and, within a very short window, be at a museum or a historical site or a pier, or any number of experiences. We could trace the footsteps of Paul Revere, or walk by a church where a placard announced that George Washington had worshipped there. On any given day we would see scientists and pass by biotechnology firms and hear people talking about their tech start-ups. Our younger child has now lived his first five years in rural Kentucky. Here, it takes hours to travel to a city, and a pier is a good day's drive away. We don't run into many people doing high-tech start-ups, and although there are plenty of historical sites, they tend to all be log cabins. While schools in urban areas can take students on short field trips, or bring in a wide range of guest speakers, these experiences can be far harder to access in rural areas, especially depending on the remoteness of one's location. These differences can be compounded by our three forces: Do students have the financial resources to take trips? Are there people moving into the location who bring with them a different world knowledge? Do local leaders understand the importance of building knowledge and experiences? Let's keep this big picture in mind as we consider three major lessons for rural reading instruction.

Lesson 1: Learn More About Local Language

In the epilogue of *Preventing Reading Difficulties*, the authors wrestle with long-term reading outcomes for middle school students from cultures that have not historically succeeded at school.[29] The authors concluded that current methods of instruction are not effective at teaching language skills beyond decoding. They argue that a new type of culturally relevant instruction is needed: one in which teachers are trained to understand students' different language backgrounds and how they might make reading accessible, purposeful, and engaging for these students.

Children raised as storytellers have an appreciation of language that often remains an untapped reservoir of knowledge. However, accessing this knowledge is not as simple as asking a child to tell a story when there are big differences between the types of narrative a child learns at home and the type most common in school. When Sky showed kindergartners in Appalachian Kentucky a series of pictures depicting the adventures of a family of bears, many were unable to produce a story. They simply fell silent. It seemed that the same children who were eager storytellers at home and in school hallways and lunchrooms were so unfamiliar with this more school-like narrative task, they were unable to respond to it.

In school, problems arise when the expectations for participation differ substantially from those at home. A classic work on the cultural mismatch between home and school is Sarah Michaels's description of "sharing time" in a first-grade classroom.[30] The white classroom teacher misunderstood the thematically oriented narratives of her African American students and tried to convert their talk to linear accounts that conformed to her cultural expectations. Even as first graders, the students in the study expressed frustration with the teacher and with sharing time. What might have been an opportunity to engage children in storytelling and build language skills became a source of disengagement with school.

Making print personally useful requires knowledge of the students and the language that they bring with them to school.[31] Some of the most skilled teachers we have observed are able to capitalize on the common styles of home talk to bridge children toward more school-like forms. For example, Judy Hensley, a middle school teacher in another Appalachian district in Harlan County, Kentucky, has charged her students with gathering local stories around a variety of topics, from mountain mysteries to animal encounters. She guides her students in revising oral narratives into written format, and the students ultimately publish a paperbound version of their collected stories. Her students' latest volume is over four hundred pages long. Judy is like many of the teachers we have met from the community, and her familiarity with student lives is certainly an advantage in undertaking such complex work. Nevertheless, an outsider can gain an understanding of local styles with some deliberate work. Anthropologist Shirley Bryce Heath has long encouraged teachers to embark on their own ethnographic work in local communities in order to better understand local "ways with words." Teachers who do not share the same cultural background may particularly benefit from explicitly engaging in study of different language forms with their students.[32]

Lesson 2: Connect with Community-Based Organizations and Experiences

It is important to tap into local resources, from a 4-H club run by a county extension agency to the local governing body of a Native nation. Community organizations and their leaders can play a major role in diminishing some of the disconnects between home and school that have been documented in the literature.[33] Moreover, the school staff we have worked with were excited by the idea of connecting with an institution central to their community. Rural communities may not have the programs that first come to mind when helping students, such as nonprofit-operated afterschool programs (e.g., City Year, Big Brothers Big Sisters), but a closer look at the places where community members invest time and energy may reveal an unexpected source of school support.

For example, in rural Appalachian Kentucky, church plays a significant role in all children's lives, whether through sermons, Sunday School, or actual Bible lessons conducted at school. Therefore, all children, regardless of church attendance, had some level of interaction with faith-based messages and language. A large majority of children appeared to have substantial exposure to religious ideas and messages, and spent a great deal of their out-of-school time involved in church activities. In these families, prayers were said at several moments throughout the day, Bible verses were recited, and life's lessons were translated through scripture. Therefore, religion appeared to be one of the most powerful channels of literacy in the community.

But even more important than connecting with community organizations is building from community strengths and experiences. This represents a great deal of the passion we brought up early in the chapter. Once you are embedded in a rural community, you begin to know the culture and traditions. You can quickly make connections to what is relevant to students. You can begin to anticipate their difficulties and plan around them. Although it is a lot of work, it also represents the art of teaching—an art that is often too easily lost in an age that is focused on data and accountability. Strong leaders will be able to implement this work. In the best case scenarios, they can even help students use language to reimagine their communities.

Lesson 3: Teach Language

The recommendation to teach language—and especially to teach academic language—is often interpreted as a recommendation to teach vocabulary. All too often this results in a small selection of single words that we want students to understand and use. This is certainly a piece of language teaching, but teaching only vocabulary would barely scratch the surface of what it truly means to teach academic language.

In fact, evidence suggests that teaching students vocabulary alone is not enough to improve their comprehension or production of texts. To understand what we read also requires knowledge of the many other words in the text, which in academic texts can quickly add up to a list far too extensive to explicitly teach students. Not only that, we have to help students understand the way that academic language is structured, from the sentence structures that organize words to the organization of ideas. Of course, this may seem puzzling given the large number of developmental studies that have found a strong positive relationship between a child's knowledge of vocabulary and her reading comprehension skill. One explanation for this is that vocabulary, because it is acquired alongside all of this other language, is a good indication of what a child knows more generally about the broader language system. This is why, to accomplish advanced literacy, we must teach our students to understand and to produce language at the word level, within sentences, and as part of larger texts. This means that instruction should explicitly teach vocabulary and the other components of the language system.

This kind of language teaching is not business as usual in most classrooms. Actually, evidence suggests that we don't spend much time teaching these skills and thus students have limited exposure to academic language and minimal experiences using it.[34] From kindergarten through twelfth grade, there are important ways that we can and should help all students to develop these skills. The only way to do this is to spend more time building their oral and written language skills—simultaneously developing their specialized knowledge about both language and the world.

If language and vocabulary skills are the key mediators of reading achievement, we also need to do a great deal of work to make sure that we are building deep conceptual knowledge of a topic. When we undertake a unit of study on big ideas like "survival," we help students learn not only the academic word *survive*, but also all of the abstract words around it that are needed to fully grasp the meaning. Units of study are a particularly rich opportunity to first find out what students already know about a topic and then help them to learn far more. In fact, this approach to teaching may be even more important for our rural students.

Very often schools are central to the rural communities they serve, providing both tremendous opportunity and responsibility to promote healthy outcomes for students. By understanding our students' home styles of talking, connecting with local agencies, and teaching language, we can make our work as reading teachers relevant to our students' lives. In the next chapter, we will talk about STEM—science, technology, engineering, and math—subjects that can represent new ways of talking and interacting. Even in these academic disciplines, we can use students' home style of language to bridge to new opportunities.

6

STEM Education in
Rural Communities

SINCE THE BEGINNING of home electrification, rural communities
have lagged in the implementation of new technology. In the 1930s
only 3 percent of farm homes had access to electricity. It took a
series of executive orders and acts of Congress, most notably the
Rural Electrification Act of 1936, before a majority of rural households and farms had electricity. In the 1950s and 1960s, access to
the telephone in rural communities followed a similar path. As we
shared in chapter 1, the challenge of today is an enormous digital divide affecting rural communities' access to the internet and
mobile service. Yet the wave of new technology came with more
than challenges in implementation; the internet age has coincided
with a seismic shift in the US economy.

Not only are rural communities falling behind in access to
the internet, but they also must meet the challenge of educating
students for a technology and health-care-driven services-based
economy. This has put tremendous pressure on middle and high
schools to educate students in the areas of science, technology,
engineering, and math (STEM). More recently, the importance of

arts education in design thinking and creativity has been added to the mix, creating the acronym STEAM.

As the internet became firmly embedded in the lives of people and daily business in the early 2000s, it became abundantly clear that the technology boom was not going away. There was a sharp increase in the demand for anyone trained in engineering, software development, or other technology-related fields. Many universities established introductory computer science classes that covered beginning programming for students majoring in any subject. By 2005, nearly a third of college freshmen said they intended to major in a science or engineering-related field.[1] That number continued to rise, and by 2011 more than 40 percent of freshmen said they wanted to major in science or engineering.[2] That year, President Barack Obama declared that the rise of technology and the shifting labor market was a "Sputnik moment" for the country, and required investment in education.[3] At the same time, data from cross-national tests, such as the Program for International Student Assessment (PISA), showed US students falling further behind other countries in science and math.

The National Science Foundation had started using the acronym STEM as early as 2001.[4] But the term did not really catch on until the end of the decade. With the support of private philanthropy, states began allocating funds to schools for STEM educational efforts. One of the first was Ohio, which launched the STEM Learning Network in 2008 with support from the Bill & Melinda Gates Foundation.[5] The $30 million investment launched seven hubs and training centers statewide and created twenty new schools, all with the goal of infusing and disseminating STEM literacy into teaching and learning.[6] Other states, including Kentucky, West Virginia, and Idaho, followed similar investments in STEM education.[7] As STEM efforts and funding ramped up, there were concerns that arts and humanities were being ignored, to the detriment of students.

Arts advocates argued that design thinking and creativity were just as important to twenty-first-century jobs as skills found in STEM fields.[8] By 2016, efforts to better equip students for the future incorporated arts. But whether you call it STEM or STEAM education, the ultimate goal is to revamp teaching and learning in schools so students can succeed in the future. In this chapter we use the term STEM for simplicity, but also point to examples that incorporate art, creativity, design thinking, and modeling.

In rural areas, the STEM movement came with unique challenges and opportunities. Of course, these are often amplified by the forces of economic vitality, population stability, and community leadership. In the next section, we address some of these challenges. We then identify a number of innovative efforts that have overcome barriers to provide rural students with world-class STEM experiences.

RURAL STEM CHALLENGES

Rural schools are critical to helping communities transition to the new economy, but there are some important obstacles in doing so.[9] We have already touched upon some of characteristics of rural communities that might impede efforts in STEM. One, of course, is the existing digital divide. Schools in rural communities just do not have access to the internet bandwidth now required for an entire class (let alone multiple classes) to stream video or use bandwidth-heavy digital educational programs. The Federal Communications Commission established 25 megabits per second (Mbps) as the minimum speed to qualify as broadband.[10] It goes even further in stating that individual students need at least 5 Mbps to learn effectively using online programs and tools. Educational technology experts argue that schools need at least 1.5 Mbps per device.[11] For a class of twenty all accessing the internet at the same time, the teacher would need a minimum of 30 Mbps dedicated to the classroom. With multiple classrooms online, that minimum speed easily gets above 250 Mbps for uninterrupted learning. Most students in the United States attend schools that meet these minimum requirements for connectivity. However, of those who do not have access—more than 6.5 million students—80 percent attend rural schools.[12]

A special contribution added to everyone's phone and internet bill, called the Universal Service Schools and Libraries Program or "E-rate," is supposed to help rural communities get access to high-speed internet. However, critics point out that the program is underfunded, especially when the cost to install broadband in rural areas is often more than double that elsewhere.[13] Private companies have little incentive to build the necessary infrastructure in communities where the population is dwindling, or in those experiencing economic decline. Vast distances and rugged terrain make the disconnect between the expense of the project and the possible payoff even greater.

Many rural schools adapt to the limited broadband by downloading programs overnight, then working in groups during the day so only a few computers in each class are online at a time, or staggering online time throughout the school with a master schedule. These workarounds at least give students minimum access to the online programs they need for STEM-related activities. The real problem is if they need to complete any of the computer-based or online work at home.

According to a Pew research report, one-sixth of families with school-aged children do not have access to high-speed internet at home.[14] Most of these children are from low-income backgrounds; nearly one-third of families earning below $50,000 do not have high-speed internet.[15] Online access at home for rural African American and Hispanic students is even more grim; in remote rural communities 41 percent of African American students and 26 percent of Hispanic students have no internet access or only dial-up at home.[16]

This lack of access has led to a "homework gap" where students without adequate internet access are unable to complete assignments or do schoolwork from home.[17] One study found that due to lack of access, nearly 50 percent of students were unable to complete a homework assignment and 42 percent said they received a lower grade.[18] This may sound like the twenty-first-century version of "the dog ate my homework" excuse, but the challenge is real in rural communities. Consider the experiment that Doug Napier, a rural high school information technology teacher, conducted with his students. Using inexpensive do-it-yourself computer kits—Raspberry Pis—Napier's students tested the real-time internet speeds across their community, including in many of their homes.[19] Of the nearly seventy readings in the community, most recorded speeds of only 1 to 9 Mbps, far less than the 25 Mbps that meet the guidelines of "broadband."[20] A lack of services came into stark view in the early spring of 2020, when schools across the country had to close their doors in response to the coronavirus epidemic. Moving learning online was not possible for many rural schools; in other cases students and their teachers struggled to complete the semester.

Lack of access to high-speed internet in rural schools and homes has real consequences on student outcomes. Those students who do not have access to high-speed internet at home score lower in critical STEM subjects such as math and science.[21] The divide also has implications for students' future career opportunities. As Allen Pratt, executive director for the National Rural Education Association, wrote, "Without broadband connectivity, kids living in rural areas are being prepared to compete in a 21st Century economy with 20th Century tools."[22]

There is another key challenge to providing STEM education in rural communities: they have neither the numbers nor the concentration of role models in STEM-related fields. Jobs in the technology sector are a hallmark of a vital economy, so this can be a particular problem in rural communities declining in economic vitality, population, or both. Rural students' understanding of what a software developer, graphic designer, videographer, electrical engineer, architect, or biologist does is often limited to what they can learn from the internet. For example, in the rural communities we have lived there is often only one architect, one software developer, or one electrical engineer for a hundred-mile radius around the community.

This scarcity of experience often extends into instruction, where many rural teachers in STEM-related fields do not have formal training in the area. For example, software development classes in rural communities are often taught by teachers who have a passion or strong interest in programming but may not necessarily have a degree in computer science. This can be seen in the lack of Advanced Placement (AP) courses in STEM subjects found in rural areas, which require teachers with deep subject knowledge. Research has shown that rural students have significantly less access to AP STEM courses; 62 percent of rural schools offer at least one AP STEM course, compared with 93 percent of suburban schools.[23]

As we'll discuss in depth in the next chapter, this lack of exposure also influences students' perceptions of future careers. Encouragement from adults to explore STEM experiences is one of the most predictive factors in whether a student pursues a STEM-related career.[24]

Despite the lack of access to adequate technology and role models in STEM fields, rural communities still have just as strong a desire for STEM education as their urban and suburban counterparts. A survey conducted by Google found that 82 percent of parents and 68 percent of teachers in rural America said that teaching computer science was as important or more important than traditional subjects such as math, history, and English.[25] For their part, students in rural communities were just as likely as their urban and suburban peers to say they wanted to learn STEM subjects, such as computer science, and that doing so would be important for their future careers.[26]

With the acknowledged need to provide quality STEM education to students, rural schools—often in collaboration with the private sector—have launched innovative programming to meet these challenges.

INTERNET-ENABLED STEM EDUCATION

In the last decade, a number of innovative programs, courses, schools, and partnerships have been launched to meet the need of rural STEM education. One of the first to emerge was Microsoft's Technology Education and Literacy in Schools (TEALS) program, started in 2009. The goal of TEALS is to build teacher capacity and student interest in computer science and technology.[27] TEALS partners with high schools, providing them an established curriculum with introductory and AP courses in computer science as well as instructional support from volunteer software engineers. To meet the needs of rural schools, TEALS developed a specialized remote conferencing system requiring a bandwidth speed of only 2 Mbps per user to connect experienced computer science professionals with teachers and students.[28] The program has been deployed successfully in many rural communities, which contain about 20 percent of all participating schools. For example, in a very rural high school not far from where we live, the TEALS program has led more than 20 percent of students to take computer science.[29]

Just a year prior to the launch of TEALS, in 2008, Salman Khan launched Khan Academy on YouTube. The engaging video tutorials and lessons combined with the simplicity of the YouTube platform quickly made Khan Academy popular with students. By 2015, lessons covered everything from algebra to the French Revolution, and more than six million students a month watched them.[30] Rural school districts also found value in Khan Academy early on to provide personalized learning in math. For example, in 2012 the state of Idaho launched the largest pilot project at the time to bring Khan Academy to 570 classrooms serving nearly thirteen thousand students across six hundred miles of rural communities.[31] More recently, Khan Academy has partnered with the College Board—maker of the SAT—to provide SAT tutoring to rural students across the United States.[32]

Of course, there are numerous virtual and online courses and schools that enroll many rural students. Rural schools often rely on online education for AP or foreign language courses when it's hard to fill an entire class or find a qualified instructor. Indeed, online K–12 education overall has grown significantly over the last decade, with nearly three million students taking some form of online class in 2019.[33] Students can also attend public school entirely online through providers such as Keystone, K12, and Laurel Springs. These examples highlight the important ways that online classes expand opportunities for rural students when the problem of bandwidth is resolved.

STEM LEARNING COMMUNITIES AND PARTNERSHIPS

There are also a few established STEM curriculum providers that are popular in rural communities. One of these, Project Lead the Way (PLTW), has been around since 1997. PLTW incorporates real-world applied learning experiences in its comprehensive computer science, engineering, and biomedical science curricula. We often see PLTW in rural communities because of the in-depth professional development and classroom support teachers receive during implementation. PLTW also has experience working closely with rural school districts, which represent more than 20 percent of their customers. That said, the one big drawback with the program for many rural school districts is the cost. PLTW in rural areas is often supported by philanthropy and implemented through consortiums or cooperatives composed of multiple school districts. For example, a foundation in rural Illinois helped a consortium of four school districts and twenty-six schools implement PLTW.[34] Similarly, Chevron gave millions of dollars to dozens of rural schools in southwestern Pennsylvania, northern West Virginia, and eastern Ohio for PLTW.[35] In these examples, strong leadership and ample financial resources provided rural students with exceptional STEM programming.

For many rural schools and districts, providing high-quality STEM education for students goes beyond a budgetary issue. Sifting through the dozens of curricula and services can be overwhelming, especially if no one has a strong background in STEM curricula or if the available expertise is only within one area. To overcome this challenge, many school districts have joined learning communities that focus on STEM education. One of the biggest is STEM Ecosystems, which helps facilitate more than eighty-four learning communities across the United States.[36] Many of these, such as the North Dakota STEM Ecosystem and the Ohio Valley STEM Cooperative, serve rural areas. The goal of the learning communities is to form cross-sector partnerships that identify rich STEM learning experiences both in school and out of school as well as equip educators so they deliver high-quality STEM education. The New Tech Network is another provider of STEM-focused learning communities.[37] The nonprofit helps schools design project-based learning that emphasizes relevance, critical thinking, and creativity. Their approach has shown to be quite successful with rural schools.[38] Programs like this are particularly promising because they address student needs while simultaneously building the capacity of local leaders to understand issues, collaborate, and solve problems.

In rural communities, universities and colleges tend to be the most likely partners for STEM educational efforts. Some partnerships focus on teacher professional development in STEM; others might offer student enrichment experiences in the summer or supplemental STEM learning activities. For example, the Infinity Project, a joint partnership between Southern Methodist University and Texas Instruments that provides rural teachers with instructional support, materials, and curriculum design in areas of engineering.[39] Vanderbilt University in Tennessee has a field trip program and summer science academy for rural students as well as a teacher training program to support STEM education.[40] Another university in Tennessee, Roane State, partners with businesses to provide Lab-in-a-Box kits that supply materials and lesson plans to rural school districts.[41] In New England, Dartmouth College helped create new science and engineering programs for middle and high school students in rural New Hampshire and Vermont.[42]

In general, university partnerships can accelerate STEM teacher professional development in rural school districts, especially when new learning technologies emerge, such as 3D printing, build-a-computer kit, or robotics. That said, these partnerships are very often funded by grants with limited timelines. So, while they are an important component of building STEM capacity in rural school systems, they should not be viewed as a sustainable solution. The learning communities that many rural schools do use to embed STEM into daily instruction are often rural educational cooperatives.

Rural educational cooperatives (RECs) are groups of individuals (community and business leaders, educators, principals, administrators, school board members) and organizations (school districts, economic development agencies, local colleges and universities) who collaborate to improve educational opportunities for rural students.[43] A typical REC has ten to thirty-five school districts located contiguously in a geographic region of a rural state. They have been around for decades in rural education; many formed in the 1980s to increase buying power when purchasing textbooks, curricula, and technology. Over the years, RECs have expanded their focus beyond purchasing power to include resource sharing, advocacy, joint curriculum design, college and career readiness, and comprehensive strategic implementation.[44] The Golden Triangle Cooperative in North Central Montana, for example, supports more than fifty public and private schools with curriculum design, program assessment, and teacher professional development. It also holds an annual summer institute for teachers that includes sessions on how to integrate STEM into all subjects and better use instructional technology.[45] The Ohio Appalachian Collaborative involves twenty-seven school districts in rural southeast Ohio. Together, they defined four model pathways for students that align directly with business sectors in the region. The STEM pathway includes dual-credit courses to prepare students for technical and engineering careers.[46] These programs are critical for building community leadership.

Near our home community, the Kentucky Valley Educational Cooperative (KVEC) is composed of twenty-two school districts serving over fifty thousand students and three thousand educators.[47] Founded in 1969, KVEC garnered national attention in recent years for its STEM educational efforts. In 2014, it received a $30 million Race to the Top grant to complete one of the largest rollouts of advanced classroom technology in a rural area.[48] More recently, KVEC launched an online social platform, The Holler, to connect community members and share resources.[49] Among other STEM investments, KVEC operates an Innovation Lab for district members that includes a STEM maker space and virtual reality capture suite. KVEC and The Holler also host an annual conference where hundreds of local teachers present innovative instructional practices.[50] KVEC's efforts have attracted visits and funding from Bill and Melinda Gates, Mark Zuckerberg, and Howard Schultz. For local high school teacher Colby Kirk, KVEC offered tremendous benefits in teaching his students STEM concepts. His students participated in a drone program with students from ten other schools in the region. As a part of the competition, his students had to design and build a drone that then competed with other schools in constructing and then racing their inventions. All the materials, curriculum, and travel to the competition were free because Kirk's school was a member of KVEC. According to Kirk, "KVEC provided one of the most memorable experiences for myself and my students, and it didn't cost us anything."

STEM MAGNET PROGRAMS AND SCHOOLS

In a number of rural states, one strategy to provide exceptional STEM education is through application-based residential public high schools, typically in partnership with a flagship public university. The North Carolina School for Science and Mathematics, the nation's first residential public high school, serves students in nearly all counties in the state through its residential and online programs. The school has emerged as a world leader in secondary science and engineering education, offering courses in machine learning, biomedical engineering, and quantum mechanics.[51] Its students rank number one worldwide for winners of the Siemens Competition in Math, Science, and Technology, and it is the number two high school in the nation for semifinalist appearances in the Intel Science Talent Search.[52] The school also has feeder programs with its STEM Scholars Program and K-9 STEM Enrichments. The Scholars Program, for ninth and tenth graders, delivers enhanced computer science and math-enriched STEM elective courses delivered through interactive video conferencing.[53] The K-9 Enrichments are supplemental interactive video lessons designed to augment classroom curriculum with hands-on activities in computer science, biomedical engineering, and food science tracks.[54]

Since the founding of the North Carolina School for Science and Mathematics, residential public high schools have launched in Alabama, Arkansas, Illinois, Indiana, Kansas, Kentucky, Maine, Massachusetts, North Carolina, Oklahoma, South Carolina, and Texas. Alabama, Mississippi, and North Carolina also have residential high schools for the arts. Here in Kentucky the Gatton Academy for Mathematics and Science accepts ninety-five students a year for its residential program on the campus of Western Kentucky University. A quarter of the students come from Appalachian Kentucky counties.[55] The Craft Academy for Excellence in Science and Math is located in northeastern Kentucky on the campus of Morehead State.[56] Both of these schools serve large numbers of rural students from all over the state, many of whom go on to attend highly selective colleges. That said, residential public high schools do get some criticism for drawing talented students away from their home communities during a critical developmental period in high school.

Some rural communities have launched their own standalone STEM schools for secondary students. These can take the form of comprehensive full-day, half-day, or school-within-a-school programs for two, three, or four years. For example, the county adjacent to where we live launched the Laurel County Schools Center for Innovation. The Center for Innovation offers STEM programs of study for juniors and seniors in health sciences, engineering technology, industrial technology, and media arts.[57] Students attend the school for a half-day, either in the morning or afternoon, earning high school credit, college credit, and certifications. For example, students in the engineering program become proficient in computer-assisted drafting (CAD), 3D print technology, and VEX robotics systems. Those in the media program learn the creative design process, camera operations, and video production with the use of a state-of-the-art production studio.[58]

PLACE-BASED EFFORTS

So far, we have focused attention on rural STEM efforts that are largely program-based or school-based. We highlighted these because they illustrate some of the best comprehensive STEM education opportunities for rural students in the United States. That said, we know that the majority of STEM efforts happen in rural classrooms and communities, facilitated by tireless teachers and local volunteers. Although rarely covered in the media or written up in foundation reports, there are numerous activities and experiences provided locally to rural students to enhance their understanding of science, technology, engineering, and math. What makes these teacher- or volunteer-led STEM activities special is that they are often embedded within the context of a community. This place-based STEM learning is powerful because it leverages student background knowledge and expertise. At Pine Mountain Settlement School, this type of place-based STEM education might find local students gathering macroinvertebrates in nearby streams, identifying them by their locally known and scientific names, and then testing a hypothesis about water quality based on the presence or absence of certain species. The farm at Pine Mountain also provides ample place-based activities to learn about soil science, organic chemical absorption in plants, and the impacts of excess nutrient runoff on waterways.

Indeed, the farms and woods of rural America have been the first experience many rural students have with the scientific process. One of the largest organizations that helps students in rural communities learn STEM through place-based experiences is the FFA, or Future Farmers of America. Founded in 1928, FFA has grown to over seven hundred thousand student members across 8,600 chapters in all fifty states, Puerto Rico, and the US Virgin Islands.[59] FFA has evolved over the decades and goes far beyond agricultural education. It provides teachers and local volunteer chapter advisors with curriculum, professional development, and resources to incorporate STEM into learning and activities. Lesson plans on biotechnology, environmental science, and mechanical engineering are available to members. At the heart of the FFA are career and leadership development competitive events where students focus on a pathway and then compete at the local, state, and national levels. Student teams can select from twenty-six different categories, including agriculture technology, floriculture, forestry, and vet science.[60] FFA also recently partnered with Microsoft to bring more technology to rural classrooms to address agricultural challenges.[61] For example, through the partnership students will have access to Microsoft FarmBeats student kits, which are pre-configured Raspberry Pi computers with temperature and humidity sensors. These cloud-based devices help students learn about technology-enabled precision agriculture.

FFA IN ACTION IN INDIANA

Bronwyn Spencer, a Purdue undergraduate who grew up on a farm in Indiana, shares how FFA helped her develop an understanding of STEM. Bronwyn says: "The integration of STEM subjects within FFA allowed me to engage with material from a technical perspective. In order to score well and win a contest, you have to understand the science, technology, engineering, and math behind the event you are competing in. During practice, my advisors took the STEM materials and put them in real-life scenarios. While preparing for the Dairy Foods Judging contest, for example, we focused on scientific processes behind milk defects. We also investigated how a defect to the mechanical build of a milker unit part would affect milk production. This was particularly beneficial for me because I personally require a hands-on approach to problem solving, and seeing the implementation of concepts helped me better understand the importance of STEM within all facets of milk production."

Bronwyn found that FFA also helped in her classes: "The presence of STEM within the FFA community helped me see an overlap within my classes taken at North Putnam High School. For example, concepts covered in honors biology relating to animal reproduction were easier to conceptualize through my experience with FFA. Since I already had some schema about the topic, it made it easier for me to understand and relate it to specific experience. I believe that being able to have these experiences actually increased my grades in STEM subjects."

Bronwyn is now majoring in elementary education. Her experiences through FFA are something that she plans to take with her to guide her own teaching career and make learning more hands-on for students.

We would be remiss not to also mention 4-H, another organization embedded in rural communities across the United States. Delivered by cooperative extensions in partnership with more than a hundred public universities, 4-H provides youth development and leadership programs for more than six million children, of whom 2.6 million are from rural communities. 4-H offers a number of STEM programs, including a weekend Maker Summit that offers mini workshops and career talks as well as curricula guides and activity kits in robotics, engineering, computer science, and environmental science.[62] For example, Sky participated in the 4-H Wildlife Habitat Evaluation Competition as a high school student. This program required students to learn about the habitat needs of specific species, then use that information to create a land management plan for a farm based on the requests of the farmer and topographical maps of the area. With more than 2,900 cooperative extension offices nationwide, 4-H represents a potential partnership in nearly every rural county.

———

STEM education is evolving as quickly as the new technologies the internet has made possible. For rural schools, getting STEM education right is about more than just the future of their students. It is also about the viability of the entire community. In the next chapter, we take a look at efforts to enhance college and career readiness for rural students.

7

College and Career Readiness

PERHAPS ONE OF THE MORE perplexing and dismal statistics you see about rural education is educational attainment. Although the number of rural students completing high school and postsecondary degrees has risen markedly over the last five decades, it lags significantly behind comparable numbers in urban and suburban communities. The reasons are complex, as we discuss in this chapter; furthermore, there is no silver bullet to getting more rural students to pursue a postsecondary degree or certification. But there are a few things we can say for certain about college and career readiness for rural students. First, rural students want to go to college just as much as their urban and suburban peers.[1] Second, having advised hundreds of Harvard College freshmen during our years in Cambridge, we firmly believe that rural students are just as capable of succeeding in college as any other students, including those from elite schools. The data on rural high school student performance also backs up that claim.[2]

In this chapter, we first unpack the statistics underlying rural student educational attainment. Using our own ethnographic research and that of others, we explain exactly why students—using their own words—choose not to persist in education beyond high school. We then show how the changing economy has led to a renaissance in career and technical education (CTE) that is benefiting rural communities all over the United States. These CTE programs, along with dual credit programs, where students can earn high school and college credit at the same time, are promising efforts in rural education that can give students the knowledge, skills, and experience they need to succeed. But first, let's look at the statistics on college and career attainment for rural students.

THE EDUCATIONAL ATTAINMENT GAP

In 1960, more than 60 percent of adults twenty-five years or older in rural areas did not have a high school diploma.[3] Of course, back then, it was more possible to get a well-paying job without finishing high school, especially in the mining, farming, or timber industries. The cost of living was also much lower; the median cost of a home was only $11,900, which in today's dollars is still only $98,000.[4] As we see over and over again, the social, cultural, and economic history and the economic vitality of rural communities have significantly shaped whether rural students pursue postsecondary education. Over the next sixty years, the high school graduation rate in rural America skyrocketed. By 2017, the percentage of adults twenty-five or older with at least a high school degree was 86 percent, and the graduation rate for rural high schools was 88 percent.[5] Indeed, the high school graduation rate in rural areas is actually higher than the US average of 85 percent.[6] Of course, it should be noted that this number masks large disparities among minorities living in rural communities. Only 77 percent of rural nonwhite students finished high school in 2017; however, this was still on par with average US high school graduation rates for African American (78 percent) and Hispanic (80 percent) students.[7] There also are pockets of persistently poor rural communities that belie the overall trend in high school graduation rates. For example, nearly 80 percent of the 467 counties where 20 percent of working adults lacked a high school diploma were rural, mostly concentrated in the Mississippi Delta, in Appalachia, and along the US-Mexico border.[8]

In general, rural students are persisting through high school graduation. The big, glaring problem, however, is that far fewer end up earning some kind of college degree. There is an enormous gap between the percentages of rural and urban/suburban students who go to college. In 2017, for example, just about half of rural people twenty-five years or older had attended some type of post-secondary education.[9] In urban areas, that figure was 62 percent, a 12-point gap. Approximately 20 percent of rural adults over twenty-five earned at least a bachelor's degree, compared with 34 percent of urban adults.[10] The more worrisome problem is that gap has widened significantly over the last twenty years. In 2000, there was a 9-point gap between rural (15 percent) and urban (26 percent) adults with a bachelor's degree. In 2017, it was 12 points, and recent data shows that it is worsening, especially for nonwhite students in rural communities.[11] We saw this firsthand at Harvard. In our ten years as undergraduate advisors and dorm parents, we worked closely with more than three hundred students. Of those, only about ten came from rural communities.

If there were bountiful dignified jobs paying a living wage for high school graduates in rural America, there might not be much cause for alarm. But, as we know, the economy has changed dramatically, and along with it the labor market. One look at any chart showing median earnings by educational attainment illustrates why it is problematic for rural students not to pursue some type of postsecondary education or training. The median annual earnings for a person with a bachelor's degree in 2018 were $62,300, with an overall unemployment rate of 2.2 percent.[12] For those with only a high school degree, the figures were $37,960 and 4.1 percent, respectively.[13] Even when you compare earnings within a rural community, there is still a considerable gap in pay by degree earned. For example, in 2017 the median earnings for high school graduates in a rural area were $29,240, compared to $42,269 for those with a bachelor's degree.

We have focused here on juxtaposing high school and a bachelor's degree simply to illustrate the widening attainment gap between rural and urban communities. Just as the economy has changed, so is postsecondary education quickly evolving. As many have noted, getting a four-year bachelor's degree may not be as relevant today as it was twenty years ago.[14] As we will discuss later in this chapter, many other postsecondary options are just as valid as a bachelor's degree, including microcredentials, certifications, and badges. But whatever postsecondary route a student takes, it is essential that he or she take one. Moreover, it is critical for rural schools to understand the importance of additional education and training beyond high school, and realize that their students are falling behind urban peers. The first step to solving the rural educational attainment gap is to understand the fundamental causes.

WHY RURAL STUDENTS DON'T GO TO COLLEGE

No simple answer explains why fewer rural students graduate from college than their urban and suburban peers. The rural educational attainment gap is wrapped in an incredibly complex puzzle that is deeply embedded in the social, cultural, and economic history of a community, and shaped by the forces of economic vitality, population stability, and community leadership. In this section, we try to peel back each layer and show how these interconnected forces impact a student's willingness to attend college and persist to graduation. As we stated at the start of the chapter, it is important to realize that rural students want to go to college as much as those in urban areas. The National Student Clearinghouse data on college enrollment shows that 59 percent of rural high school students enroll in college the following fall; the percentage of urban high school students who do so is just 3 points higher at 62 percent.[15] Furthermore, rural students appear to be equally prepared to matriculate; they score better on the National Assessment of Educational Progress than urban students, and have higher graduation rates than the national average.[16] Why, then, do far fewer rural students persist in postsecondary education? We have already seen the percentage of adults in rural areas with bachelor's degrees: 20 percent in 2017. But consider that the percentage of rural people ages eighteen to twenty-four enrolled in postsecondary education is only 29 percent, compared to 48 percent from urban areas.[17] There are a number of reasons why rural students do not stay in college after enrolling. And we want to caution against making assumptions about the driving forces of educational attainment gaps. We have seen too many errant reports that the "culture" of rural communities is the main force keeping students from going to college.

First, one clear reason rural students leave college is that they often cannot see the value of completion. With the shift in the economy, there currently is not a high concentration of jobs requiring a college degree in many rural communities. So, if a student has a strong desire to remain closer to home, as nearly all people do, then having a college degree is not a strict requirement. Indeed, a poll found that only 33 percent of rural residents considered a bachelor's degree worth pursuing, compared with 52 percent in urban areas.[18] Another oft-cited poll that came out soon after the 2016 election found similar results; 71 percent of rural white men believed colleges and universities have a role in providing skills and education, compared to 82 and 84 percent in urban and suburban areas, respectively.[19] These results often get attributed to the "culture" of rural areas when commonsense on-the-ground experience shows that there are currently not a lot of jobs for college-educated people in rural areas. Indeed, rural Americans were questioning the value of a four-year degree long before it became commonplace for students to take on mountains of debt only to work in low-paying jobs. Economic vitality is a major force in whether or not a degree can lead to expanded opportunities.

Cost is obviously another huge barrier for rural students. Average wages and median incomes are lower in rural areas. Tuition at the average four-year public university has risen over 200 percent just since 1988.[20] Meanwhile, the average hourly wages in the United States have remained flat since 1978 and in rural areas they have actually declined.[21] So, rural families literally have less and less to pay for a college education that is costing more and may not lead to a higher paying job back home. For many rural families, college just does not make economic or rational sense. Moreover, as many rural scholars have noted, there are complex family and cultural dynamics that influence postsecondary success.[22]

In rural areas, the central role of family and strong community ties draw students back home.[23] As Patricia McDonough, an education professor at UCLA, observed: "It's kind of a golden cage. You don't want to leave home, family—a way of life that you know and love."[24] We can tell you dozens of stories of rural students we have worked with in Montana, New Mexico, and Kentucky who faced pressures of the "golden cage" as students at Harvard. A colleague of ours who grew up in rural Eastern Kentucky tells of the times he phoned home to his mother about the challenges of adapting as a Harvard freshman. With each story he told of mostly typical struggles for a first-year Harvard student (e.g., demanding academic environment, living with a roommate, terrible cafeteria food), his mother would reassure him that he could always come home. His mother was reassuring him the best way she knew how, especially since neither she nor his father had attended college. That said, our colleague finally had to tell his mother to stop saying he could come home. Like many rural students who do persist and succeed in college, he could see a bigger picture of himself and the purpose of his college education.

Of course, there is also a perceptible cultural mismatch between rural communities and life at colleges and universities—even when those institutions are in a rural setting. In rural communities, common sense is often prioritized over intellectual accomplishment; lack of the former can lead to death or serious injury.[25] Smaller, tightly knit insular rural communities also sometimes develop an "us versus them" mentality that can act as a double-edged sword. On the one hand, it strengthens social bonds so that in times of need or emergency, everyone in the community gets taken care of. But it can also engender the "mistrust" of outsiders or different ways of life that higher education might represent.

Where colleges are located also contributes significantly to the educational attainment gap in rural communities. First, competitive colleges simply do not recruit in rural areas.[26] Recruiting rural students is more expensive. An admissions staff member from a highly selective private college might travel three days across eastern Wyoming, visiting nine high schools, to get twenty applicants and potentially zero admits. The only incentives for a higher education institution to dedicate resources to recruiting rural students are about assembling a diverse class of students (or, occasionally, a stellar sports team) that may eventually lead to a less polarized society. However, selective colleges do not report out the percentage of students from rural communities, much less the number of rural students who graduated from their local public high school; instead, they often report representation by state. This makes the major metropolitan areas of underrepresented states the most likely places to benefit from recruitment efforts by selective colleges

Second, students too must weigh proximity to a postsecondary educational institution. Recent reports have identified three million Americans who live in "higher education deserts" where a physical higher education campus is more than twenty-five miles away and internet speeds are not sufficient to support fully online learning.[27] Not surprisingly, 82 percent of these "complete deserts" are in rural areas.[28] If you just consider proximity to a nearby campus of public higher education, more than twelve million rural Americans live in "physical deserts."[29] Indeed, rural counties cover 97 percent of the United States, but are home to only 14 percent of the nation's colleges and universities.[30] And even when a rural community does have an institution of higher education nearby, it is often a lower-resourced community college or state school branch.[31]

Consider just how important geography and proximity are to a student's college choice. More than half (56 percent) of students at public four-year colleges grew up less than fifty miles away and the average community college student travels just eight miles to go to school.[32]

As we have shown, there are many different reasons rural students do not make it through college. In 2013, Geoff experienced the complexity of this issue when he was launching his software company, Giant Otter Technologies. The software development process required a high degree of cultural knowledge (the product was an antibullying simulation for schools) and the overseas contractors previously used were not going to be able to do the work of tagging and coding transcripts of conversations around bullying. At a Christmas family gathering, Geoff discovered that an arts nonprofit in Eastern Kentucky, Appalshop, ran a summer program to train recent high school graduates in digital media. It was suggested that alumni of that program could potentially help with the software development process. After exploring the possibility of the partnership, Geoff set up a pilot project in Eastern Kentucky and hired four recent high school graduates to work as a team. The pilot was a success, and likely influenced our return to Eastern Kentucky (though we didn't know it at the time).

To help us assess the success of the program, we decided to undertake a small research study to better understand the experiences of the team, particularly in relation to college and career opportunities. We conducted interviews of the four employees as well as some community members to learn how such projects could succeed in the future. Of the four employees, three were male and one female. All were in their twenties and all had attended college at some point, but only one had a degree.

What emerged from the interviews were themes around opportunity, the role of education, and the individual interests and talents of the team. Specifically, all employees repeatedly expressed that their jobs at Giant Otter were "unique," and unlikely to be available to others, or even themselves, in the future. Because of this, all of the employees expressed cynicism that high school, college, or a training program could or should prepare them for similar roles. "I don't expect schools or colleges to train me for this kind of work," said one of the employees directly. "This is a really unique job. There are not other jobs like this out there."[33]

Interestingly, their responses also emphasized a perception that there was not much utility for a college or high school degree. As one employee said, "School is about learning things just to learn them so you can take some standardized test." Another said it was painful to see his peers "striving for a degree they would never be able to use. You know, you put in your time, do all that aggravating work, then you end up at Walmart or [the grocery store] or in the coal mines anyway." Many interviews emphasized the dehumanizing aspects of work. As one participant said, "The only people who are willing to hire me want to put me in front of a dangerous vat of grease or otherwise destroy my body."

For three of the participants, school was in direct conflict with their most immediate and basic needs. One talked about caring for his dying father when he was attending a local community college: "There were times that I didn't even get to go to sleep at night; then I was supposed to stay awake all day to take a geometry class." Another said that what school "really should do is help people be part of something here that actually feeds people—and I mean that in a literal way . . . I wish there had been opportunities in school to help us grow food and eat."

All of the employees greatly enjoyed their experience working at Giant Otter and saw it as a way of engaging a part of their identity that was not often able to be expressed because the work, as one employee said, "uses my mind." Most were disappointed that the pilot project would end and that they would need to move on to other, often temporary, locations so that they could return to their only work opportunities.

For the employees in the Giant Otter pilot, leaving their rural community was not considered an option. These individuals saw their employment largely as a product of chance rather than a harbinger of the opportunities to come. As other researchers have found in rural communities, the employees did not see a connection between postsecondary training and their current or future employment opportunities. The big takeaway for us was that for postsecondary education to work for rural students, it needed to lead to real economic opportunity in home communities. This is a particularly important and difficult challenge in communities where the forces of economic vitality and population stability have led to increasingly limited professional opportunities. In the next section, we highlight some higher education efforts that are working for rural communities, including dual credit and innovative career and technical education (CTE) programs. We also explore what traditional four-year institutions could do to reach more rural students and ensure they stay to graduate.

DUAL CREDIT COURSES

Dual, or concurrent, credit courses in high school have increased dramatically over the last decade. These courses, in which students earn both high school and college credit, can smooth the transition into postsecondary education and help students prepare for the rigors of college. Because the courses are often free, dual credit can also ease the cost of attending college. Many high schools now offer dual credit and more than a third of high school students now take courses for college credit.[34]

A number of states have turned to dual credit to help boost post-secondary graduation rates for rural students. Idaho, for example, allocates $4,125 to every student in seventh through twelfth grades to pay for college classes or Advanced Placement tests.[35] Using the funds, students can graduate from high school with an associate's degree, which can then be transferred to any public state university. The program has found some success with rural students; the top fifteen participating districts all serve rural communities.[36] Rural students were also more likely to leave high school with college credit than their urban peers.[37]

In Ohio, rural school districts have taken advantage of the state's College Credit Plus program, which gives seventh to twelfth graders an opportunity to earn college credit. In 2017–2018, more than seventy-one thousand students across the state enrolled in the program, and rural students are earning the highest rate of credit.[38] The Ohio Appalachian Collaborative, the rural educational cooperative we learned about in chapter 6, has helped its district members take advantage of the program.[39] Under the College Credit Plus funding model, the student's local high school pays for tuition and books. This disadvantages rural schools, which do not have the critical mass of students to scale up funding for dual credit programs.[40] For example, one rural district spends up to $20,000 a year just on textbooks for its students.[41] The state discounts the tuition rate if the courses are taught on the high school campus, but some schools struggle to recruit teachers who are qualified to teach college-level courses. The districts in the Ohio Appalachian Collaborative addressed this challenge by applying for grants to ease the financial burden and sharing qualified teachers across districts. As one principal said, "One may have a math teacher. We have a Spanish teacher. Another may have a business teacher. They may be all over the region but we're all committed to sharing them so we can offer a full college curriculum to our students."[42] From 2012 to 2015, the number of dual-enrollment courses in districts increased from 41 to 254 and dual-enrollment credentialed teachers increased from 82 to 156.[43]

Of course, there are challenges with offering dual credit courses in rural areas. As noted, finding and retaining qualified instructors can be difficult. Dual credit instructors must typically have a master's degree or eighteen graduate-level credits in their specialty—a requirement not many high school teachers can meet.[44] Also, if there are no colleges or universities nearby, rural students are often forced to take the dual credit courses online, which can be both expensive and limited by internet access. But, if done right, dual credit has shown to have a number of benefits for students and their families, including easing the transition to college and reducing the financial burden.[45]

CAREER AND TECHNICAL EDUCATION

In 2018, President Trump signed into law the Strengthening Career and Technical Education for the 21st Century Act, which reauthorized the long-standing Perkins Act that provides funding for career and technical education (CTE).[46] The act not only sets a new vision for CTE in the United States, but also provides increased annual funding totaling nearly $1.3 billion.[47] It attempts to address the widening skills gap that employers face in the United States as well as the burgeoning student financial aid debt of over $1.5 trillion. For example, skilled jobs such as welders, electricians, and technology support specialists had more openings than workers in 2018, with 13 percent of jobs going unfilled.[48] The revamped CTE plan provides students with work-based learning pathways to earn certifications and college credit that prepare them to continue postsecondary education after high school or enter a well-paying skilled job. Apprenticeships and pre-apprenticeships are a core component of CTE and have seen rapid expansion over the past decade. According to the Department of Labor, in 2018 there were more than 585,000 active registered apprentices, 56 percent more than five years ago.[49] Of course, the apprenticeships in CTE require a close partnership with private sector businesses and organizations.

Colorado has made considerable progress supporting innovative CTE in rural communities. It overhauled its Colorado Workforce Development Council and then created a Rural Education Council to advise the commissioner of education. The council is composed of superintendents, principals, and teachers in rural districts, and helps bring about statewide collaboration on CTE. With input from rural education leaders, in 2016 the state launched the Career Development Incentive Program, which gives school districts $1,000 in incentive funds for each high school student who completes an industry credential program, internship, or apprenticeship.[50] Over one-third of the participating districts in 2017–2018 were rural.[51] A collaboration of businesses in Colorado also launched CareerWise, which is building a statewide system of apprenticeships for high-demand, high-paying jobs.[52] Taken together, these programs help address some of the inequalities that arise in underresourced rural schools and those with quickly shifting demographics. They also build community leadership.

Another promising work-based learning model that integrates both apprenticeships and dual credit, the Pathways in Technology Early College High Schools (P-TECH), actually got its start in Brooklyn, New York, as a public school partnership with IBM.[53] Students in P-TECH programs take industry-specific college courses in their junior and senior years while working internships at local employers. After graduation, students earn their associate's degree at no cost while continuing their workplace experience.

Successful P-TECH schools have launched in rural communities in Colorado, Idaho, New York, and Texas.[54] A related approach is to provide training to adults who are becoming established in their career, by providing targeted support that promotes learning without necessarily involving formal educational enrollment. You can read more in the sidebar about the Montana Artrepreneur Program, an endeavor that provides forty hours of college-level training to artists and craftsmen in the Big Sky state without requiring official coursework.

THE MONTANA ARTREPRENEUR PROGRAM

In Montana, art businesses are seen as an important part of a tourism strategy that embraces the state's cultural heritage as an asset that brings in visitors and encourages them to spend money. The Montana Arts Council, which is part of the tourism department, has developed a program that provides intensive support to artists in telling their story, marketing their goods, and developing their business strategy. The program embraces the rural identity of many who live in Montana, encouraging ways to grow a business without relying on the infrastructure or audience of a city. A competitive application is required, and participation includes a full year of monthly workshops that provide immersive training in business fundamentals. Those who have completed the program have seen an average 654 percent growth in net sales. You can read the full report on the program at https://art.mt.gov/map.

TRADITIONAL FOUR-YEAR COLLEGE EFFORTS

Traditional four-year colleges and universities are also bolstering efforts to help rural students succeed. In the past few years, the University of North Carolina, University of Georgia, Clemson University, and Texas A&M all invested in rural student recruitment and retention.[55] Some employers and foundations in rural communities are also putting together programs to help rural college graduates return to their home communities. In rural east Tennessee, the Niswonger Foundation provides a full-tuition scholarship to promising high school graduates for each year they agree to return to work in the community. The scholarship program, called Learn, Earn, and Return, also includes leadership training.[56] In Maine, the state's largest hospital created an annual scholarship of $25,000 for local college students to attend medical school, if they agree to work two years in a rural hospital in the state.[57]

An example of how Native American rural communities promote educational attainment is the network of Tribal Colleges and Universities (TCUs). Nationwide, only 14 percent of Native Americans twenty-five or older have a bachelor's degree or higher. TCUs offer options that are closer to home, lower cost, and embedded within local communities.[58] Moreover, they have an explicit focus on integrating culture and community while shifting leadership into local hands.[59] TCUs are making an associate's, bachelor's, and in some cases a master's degree more widely available to Native students. Their emphasis on zero student debt and open admissions makes a lot of sense in communities where the economic realities make degree programs more risky. And their focus on making college more welcoming is an important model for how to reduce barriers.

Some rural colleges are responding to the need to build the local community and to help train and certify a workforce for the jobs that are available. For example, our home institution, University of the Cumberlands (UC), serves a large population of first-generation and Appalachian students. University leadership has increasingly offered programs that provide direct career opportunities, and is finding ways for students to successfully complete a degree that is best structured to their goals. In 2019, Geoff piloted an entirely new kind of course at UC that was inclusive of both current students and those who had never enrolled. Called Entrepreneurship in the Real World, the class was designed to provide tools for those in skilled trades as well as those formulating business plans. One student, for example, was a luthier—a craftsman who makes stringed instruments—who was seeking to develop kits that would allow instruments to be more affordable. The class met in different towns in the Eastern Kentucky region, blending case discussion with meetings with established business owners. There was no expectation that students in the course would go on to enroll at UC. Instead, the goal was to be certified in Entrepreneurship and Small Business based on a rigorous assessment administered through Pearson.

Postsecondary training, in whatever form it takes—be it microcredentialing in areas like HVAC, or enrollment in four-year, fully accredited colleges and universities—plays a central role in reimagining the future of rural regions. Through the student experience, residents can gain new practice with technology and insight into growing sectors. In the best cases, these programs can ignite a spirit of entrepreneurism that helps grow the career opportunities of future students, making education more relevant. Building community and responding to local needs are the goals that lead us into the final section of the book—one on putting our ideas into practice and guiding policy decisions.

PART III

Moving to Action

8

Putting It Together:
A Plan for Rural Schools

PART OF OUR MISSION in writing this book is to inspire rural educators and to take the lessons of what's working in rural communities for students and families and apply them to their contexts. What would it take to improve in the areas that are so critical for rural education: early childhood, literacy, technology, STEM, and college and career readiness? We found that thinking strategically about the forces at play in a community is key. The factors of economic vitality, population stability, and community leadership help us adapt programs and services to our own unique settings. After all, rural communities encompass a wide range of people and experiences, and the needs are equally diverse.

To this end, we turn our attention to action steps for rural schools. Our approach is straightforward: we will take a journey through the chapters of this book and consolidate the information presented through a comprehensive self-assessment process that will allow you to analyze your own school or district. The first step is to identify your community and school's social and cultural history, document how current forces shape the work you do, and then map out the strengths of your particular school or district community. From there, we provide a rubric so that you can evaluate service delivery in early childhood, literacy, technology and STEM, and college and career pipelines. This will give you a starting point for identifying a problem and undertaking change following a cycle of continuous learning that has been adapted to reflect the unique strengths of rural communities.

How you undertake this process will depend on your role and goals. If you are in an education program, you may use these tools for reflection, or perhaps to evaluate your student teaching placement. If you provide services in a particular area—say, early childhood—you may focus on just this domain. However, we believe that making lasting changes requires a committed group of diverse stakeholders to come together for a common goal. The ideal group would represent the school district, key community partnerships, and families. To that end, we have specific recommendations for professional learning communities (PLCs). These PLCs represent any group of educators and/or other stakeholders who come together specifically to learn and deepen their capacity over time.[1] By the time you have finished this chapter, you should have some clear ideas on how you can make changes to improve your school in a way that aligns with rural community development.

A COMPREHENSIVE SELF-ASSESSMENT FOR RURAL SCHOOLS

We begin our journey by undertaking a process of self-examination that follows four steps. The first step is to understand how your school or district fits in the social and historical context of your community. Second is to recognize how the social and economic forces at play shape your current school and community needs. Next you'll turn to strengths and map out the assets available to your work. Finally, you will evaluate the programs currently available to

FIGURE 8.1   A comprehensive self-assessment process for rural schools

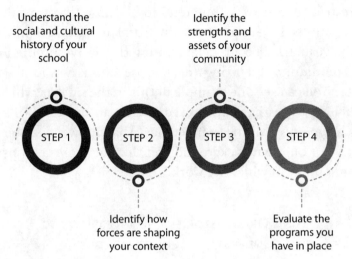

understand their strengths and weaknesses. This process, shown in figure 8.1, will help you identify a need that you can take on in the second half of the chapter.

Step 1: Understanding the Sociocultural History of Schools in Your Community

Every rural school and district is situated at a unique moment in the sociocultural history of a community. Depending on your teaching staff and community—and how difficult it may be for the people indigenous to your community to access teaching credentials—this history may be deeply familiar to school personnel or not at all. Even those of us who grow up in a community may be completely unaware of the experiences of our neighbors, since life in a community is complex and influenced by social class, race, gender, and sexual orientation. Digging into the history of a community is counter to educational initiatives that often ask us to focus specifically on what is immediate in a classroom, such as the latest test scores. But when it comes to complex organizations serving primarily rural and small communities, the ones that have the greatest success over time tend to be those that are culturally aligned.[2] Indeed, several successful rural educational initiatives over the years have begun by anchoring themselves in the history of the community and taking a deep, close look at how local schools operate.[3] You can see one example of this in the sidebar, which tells how oral histories have been used to inform practice. This work builds a type of "cultural competence" that allows us to be more reflective of our own background and then be more responsive to the community in which we work.[4]

USING ORAL HISTORIES AND INTERVIEWS TO UNDERSTAND SCHOOL HISTORY

Oral histories are one strategy to bring greater detail and understanding to how forces have shaped schooling over time. This could involve having students create oral histories that are specific to the role of schooling in the community, as has been done by organizations like Foxfire. But it could also get teachers, especially those in teacher training programs, to take a closer look at their community. When we were teachers, getting our master's degrees at Western New Mexico University, one of our required activities was to interview someone from the community who could speak to the history of the school. Sky will never forget interviewing another teacher who was Navajo and had grown up in the area. This teacher explained that in the 1970s the foster care system was used to remove her from her home—she lived in a one-room Hogan [a traditional Navajo dwelling that is still common today] that was deemed unsuitable—and send her to live with a white family in Salt Lake City, Utah, when she was just six years old. Almost as soon as she arrived, this young girl was taken to a school of white students who spoke English, when her only language was Diné.

On that first day of school, the other students tied her up to the fireman pole during recess and danced around her. It took her years to realize that they were pantomiming the Native American war whoops and dancing they had seen in movies. To her young mind their actions were inexplicable and terrifying. And when recess ended, they all ran in, leaving her there alone on the playground. That became her first memory of school: tied up, alone, and afraid on an empty playground in an unfamiliar town without the language skills to help navigate the situation.

This interview was a very formative experience for Sky, who did not understand how recently young children had been separated from their families or how difficult or traumatic some of the current experiences of school had been for people in her school community. In this case, the interview was about the legacy of the town, but interviews like these can also be very helpful in understanding immigrant experiences. These types of interviews are particularly useful when the teacher is a cultural outsider.

PLC Investigation: Create a Timeline

Bring your PLC together to create a timeline documenting the history of schooling in your community. There are several ways to accomplish this history, and it could be done quickly in groups, at one hour-long meeting, or involve a community-wide group over days or weeks. You may even choose to involve students in the process. The important part is not to simply capture the milestones of schools opening and closing, but to try and understand the specific role that schooling has played in the community over time.

We would argue that the simplest route to this type of understanding is to focus specifically on how schools did or did not intersect with the jobs and work of the community. This type of approach helps us understand how economic forces have shaped the way schooling is done. It also helps us see the ways that school has or has not been meaningful to people's livelihood, and who has been included and excluded. For example, in coal towns in the mountains of Appalachia, it behooved the coal company to limit the education of the community members, and so in an era when the private industry in a town was usually tasked with building the schools, companies made little investment. Understanding histories like these allows all of us to be more aware of our interactions and connections in our setting and to take a big-picture view.

As you create a history of your school, we suggest asking these questions:

- What have been the most influential or consequential periods in our community's history? How have these been tied to changes in our local economy and the jobs available?
- When did people begin to attend school and why? Who attended school and why?
- What have been the major employers or sources of income in our community? What type of education or degree did they require?

Step 2: Understanding the Forces at Work in Your Community

In chapter 3 we described three forces that shape rural schools today—each of these emerging from the social and cultural history of the community. These forces shape the larger context and have a big impact on how schools can operate and on the needs of the people they serve. Let's take a moment to review each of these:

1. *Economic vitality: The condition of the economy*

Economic vitality tells us about the condition of the local or regional economy. In places with a vibrant economy, jobs are available in a number of different industries, allowing community members to earn a living wage doing dignified work. In contrast, in communities with a stagnating economy, many people have a hard time finding work. Or, there are only a limited number of jobs in very specific industries. In general, rural communities struggle when only one industry has created the majority of the jobs.[5] Poor working conditions, lack of autonomy at work, and irregular work hours have all been shown to create stress on families, especially those with small children.[6] Not having work at all is connected to social isolation and depression, and is also associated with children's struggles to gain academic skills.

Schools need to be aware that the economic vitality of a community has a big influence on the stressors that families face. Lack of money creates a chain reaction of difficulties in accessing transportation, health care, childcare, and leisure. Again and again research has shown that a child's economic background plays the biggest role in his or her success in school.[7] This is even more true when many people in a community live in poverty.[8]

2. Population stability

Rural communities in transition face special issues and challenges that differ from places that have a stable population over time. When people think of rural communities, they often imagine towns with abandoned buildings and young people who can't wait to leave, as blue-collar jobs in agriculture and resource extraction become increasingly mechanized. As fewer and fewer people can find work, enrollment in schools declines and people in the community may be dealing with economic hardship or instability. In this scenario, one of the threats confronting the community is whether or not the town and school will survive.[9]

Of course, there are many different types of rural communities, including some that face population loss while others experience the very opposite—large population booms. If a new manufacturing or processing plant is built in a town, for example, it can lead to an explosion of growth, as happened in a rural Arkansas community that became home to a meat processing plant.[10] In this case, the families who came to fill the positions were immigrants. Their cultural and linguistic background was completely different from that of the people who had previously been living in the town. A sudden influx of immigrants certainly can put a great deal of stress on a school. It takes time to learn the best practices of serving a new group of students who have had different experiences of school and are still learning English.

Yet another situation some rural communities face is a population that waxes and wanes based on seasonal patterns. In chapter 5 we heard from a principal of an elementary school in Eastern Washington in a town that is best known for its stone fruit and apple orchards. Cherries are picked in the late spring and early summer, while apples are picked in the fall, and seasonal farm workers add to the town's population. Seasonality can also have a big impact on rural resort towns, where the summer months (or ski season) may have a boom of visitors coming to spend money, but the off-season sees many of those customers leave and businesses close.

3. *Community leadership*

Leadership can be transformative to a town or community, no matter how difficult the circumstances or how steep the decline it has endured. Leadership, like anything else, is nurtured or stifled by the environment. If young adults face difficult decisions around leaving home to pursue better opportunities, they are less likely to engage as leaders. If outside organizations have created power structures that minimize local leadership, then communities may not be identifying their own promising youth and nurturing them into leadership positions.[11] We suspect that we might find additional struggles with leadership in rural resort towns. Although their economy and population may be growing, powerful individuals who are new to the town—or only there during the recreation season—may create unusual competition for leadership roles and business opportunities. Those from the town may feel like they cannot take a leadership role as an increasing amount of wealth is needed to participate in government and business. Interests in tourism may redirect attention and resources away from the day-to-day needs of a community, such as schools and affordable housing.

As we think about leadership, we need to be aware that leadership styles can take different manifestations depending on cultural styles. Distributed leadership is when groups with different perspectives form and connect various resources, often without relying on a single figurehead. The goal is to find ways to support individuals so that anyone taking on a position is guided toward good decision-making with appropriate checks and balances.[12] This kind of balance is complex when there is a history of some groups holding power over others.

PLC Investigation: Conduct a "Data Walk"

To better understand the economic vitality and other forces at work in your community, we recommend taking a "data walk." This is a common approach that involves displaying information on key issues in the community in a way that makes it visible and accessible to the group. Data might be written on chart paper, or printed in large format. (See table 8.1.) Examples might include the number of children who receive free or reduced-price lunch, the number of children who passed a kindergarten readiness screener, and the percentage of students who graduate. We have participated in data walks that have included other big issues facing a community: for example, the number of children who live with grandparents, the number of children who are homeless, and the percentage of children attending preschool. A facilitator can provide sticky notes for participants to write down their reactions and observations and post them next to the data.

Step 3: Mapping Your Strengths

Rural communities are places of rich history and culture, of beautiful natural surroundings and residents who fiercely protect these gifts. Those of us who choose a rural life do not need convincing

TABLE 8.1   Forces at work in your community

Use this table to help your PLC identify how three key forces are shaping the work in your community.

FORCE	QUESTIONS FOR YOUR PLC	PLC RESPONSES
Economic vitality	• Who are the families living in poverty? Why are they in poverty? • What are the major employers in town? Who works in them?	
Population stability	• Do you live in a community that is growing or declining? What is driving that change? • Who lives in your community now? • Who are the primary groups that the school needs to serve? Does that population of students match the population of teachers?	
Community leadership	• Who are the leaders in the community? • What organizations do they represent? • Who are the leaders in the school? Consider both the formal leaders and the informal ones. Do you have a school secretary who is the main touchpoint with parents? What about major coaches? Are there teachers who serve as mentors?	

that there are numerous benefits. But when we think of schooling, specifically, it helps to orient ourselves around strengths that have been identified in research. These evidence-based assets allow us to be strategic about our planning for successful education initiatives. Looking across the research done in rural communities, we identified four common strengths: greater socioeconomic and racial integration, strong teaching force and schools, deep community social networks, and a connection to place. Of course, how these manifest in specific communities varies, so let's look more closely at each one.

- *Strength 1: Greater socioeconomic and racial integration*

We previously touched on Raj Chetty's work that found rural communities provide greater social mobility than their urban counterparts. If you distill this work, it shows that you have a greater chance to make more money in your lifetime than your parents if you grow up in a rural community. This finding is remarkable given that many rural communities cannot offer the range of professional roles that can be found in cities. But in fact, some research shows that the more rural your background, the greater your opportunity to advance or attain leadership in your job.[13] Of course, that does not mean that all rural communities allow mobility or do not struggle with serious issues of segregation around race and social class. Cynthia Duncan has written about the differences between rural communities that were persistently poor versus other rural communities that weathered economic change and adapted to create opportunity.[14] The most successful rural communities were those that were the most egalitarian and civic-minded. This sets a great example of how rural communities should embrace mobility and integration as potential strengths that can be activated to promote student achievement.

- *Strength 2: Strong teachers and schools*

Rural students do better on national performance assessments than their peers of the same social class in urban and suburban schools. And it appears that one major reason for these better outcomes is a well-trained and experienced teaching force. Of course, some rural schools struggle with teacher shortages, or have a hard time recruiting teachers in specific areas such as science or special education. Also, shifting populations may make it hard to have teachers who represent the linguistic and cultural background of all students. But the strongest rural schools have a teaching force and staff who help students feel welcomed, involved, and understood. Investment in teachers and leaders pays off over time because most will continue to work in the school or district for a significant period of time.

- *Strength 3: Strong, deep, and stable family ties and social networks*
  Powerful and lasting relationships are one of the keys that enable children to navigate challenges over time and come out resilient.[15] The incredibly robust and interdependent ties within rural school communities have been highlighted by a number of researchers.[16] The connectedness within a rural school can be a major source of strength for students. Given that social networks extend beyond the school walls, we also need to think about the potential for partnering with a variety of organizations. For example, cooperative extension agencies, churches, and other local organizations all provide the potential for building relationships with rural youth.

- *Strength 4: A deep connection to place*
  Rural students have an especially deep connection to the places they are from. There is often a strong connection to nature, to social and cultural traditions, and to a shared heritage. Some of the most innovative teaching pedagogy has used place-based approaches that draw on these connections to guide inquiry and give students opportunities to solve real-world problems affecting their own communities.

PLC Investigation: Create an Asset Map
As your group gathers, you can create an "asset map" that highlights the strengths of your school or district in relation to the list we have identified here. Asset maps take a variety of forms: they can be plotted on an actual map of a community to mark where resources

are in physical space. They can be webs or concept maps that show the relationships between areas and programs. Or, they can simply be a list.

We invite your PLC to use table 8.2 to help you identify the assets in your community. Begin by brainstorming and listing strengths you see in your own school or district. The next step is to identify other organizations or community leaders that provide services and resources to students and add those to the list. These might include nearby community colleges or universities, community-minded businesses, civic organizations, hospitals or clinics, and so on. As you go through this exercise, keep in mind that you will be looking at some of the programs you already have

TABLE 8.2   Identifying assets in your community

Use the chart to help you identify the assets of your community that align with the identified overarching strengths of rural communities.

RURAL COMMUNITY STRENGTH	EXAMPLES OF ASSETS IN OUR SCHOOL AND COMMUNITY	ORGANIZATIONS, PROGRAMS, AND LEADERS THAT ENHANCE THIS ASSET
Social and economic integration		
Strong teachers and schools		
Strong, deep, and stable family ties and social networks		
Connection to place		

in place. This list will give you ideas on how to expand the work and build capacity in specific areas.

Step 4: Evaluating Programming Already in Place

In part II of this book, we talked about four educational areas where rural schools can have an impact on their communities— early childhood, rural literacy, STEM, and CTE and links to careers and technology. It would be incredibly challenging for any small or rural school to deliver excellent programming in all of these areas. But it is useful to establish where you stand in each so that you can identify opportunities to reach new kids or perhaps expand your work in a way that could be impactful for your community.

PLC Investigation: Use a Rubric

Rubrics are useful tools for deciding areas of relative strength or weakness. Use the rubric in table 8.3 to help you see whether the work in this area is emerging, established, or sustaining in relation to the models we have shared in this book. The highest capacity programs build collaboration among families and programs and help further the community as a whole. Less effective programs take place in isolation within the walls of a school. Identify how your school or district would score in the program areas that are relevant to your work.

LEADING SCHOOL IMPROVEMENT

Now that you have had an opportunity to reflect on your own school and the economic and social forces at play, as well as the strengths of your resources and programming, you are well positioned to undertake a school-improvement process. There are many great resources out there on creating school improvement plans. One of our favorites is the PELP Problem-Solving Framework

TABLE 8.3 A program evaluation rubric

AREA	EMERGING	ESTABLISHED	SUSTAINING
Early childhood	Some preschool programming takes place at the school, but most children begin their school experience in kindergarten.	There is collaboration among the preschools in town. The school shares training and resources with Head Start and perhaps private centers as well.	A formal network or committee connects various stakeholders in early childhood education and care. These include home-based care, private day care, Head Start, and preschool through the local elementary school, as well as pediatricians and service providers. This group shares resources and comes together to support local families in need.
Literacy	There is a set literacy curriculum and some understanding that literacy instruction must extend beyond elementary grades, but the primary focus of literacy instruction remains on decoding in elementary grades.	There is a coordinated effort to increase literacy skills across all grade levels, including in the content areas in middle and high school. A strong system is in place to support struggling readers, beginning with early identification in the primary grades.	Literacy is a focus of all grade levels and content areas, with an emphasis on how we foster language as a way for students to access new identities and possibilities. There is a clear understanding of the types of talking and interacting that may be unfamiliar to our specific students, and we help those students learn new behaviors and the appropriate times to apply their knowledge.

(continued)

TABLE 8.3   A program evaluation rubric (*continued*)

AREA	EMERGING	ESTABLISHED	SUSTAINING
Technology & STEAM	The school offers all of the necessary science classes for postsecondary education. Technology is integrated into isolated projects in different classrooms.	Technology infrastructure, including equipment and network capacity, have received explicit focus from school leaders. For example, Chromebooks may be available to groups of students along with the internet connectivity needed to make them usable. Technology is widely available and this has led to some exciting collaborations and opportunities.	Technology is accessible to all students and equipment and network speeds all meet requirements needed for advanced use. Special programs are available for advanced technology use where appropriate. Technology is used to expand connections and opportunities for students, including options to take classes not available in the school and to build technical skills.
College and career pipelines	Graduation requirements are clear to instructional leaders and school guidance staff. Major barriers to graduation, such as attendance, have received attention. A career fair or guest speakers allow students to hear about opportunities.	The school offers internships and placements that allow career exploration before graduation. There are partnerships in place with local community and technical colleges and four-year colleges to allow dual enrollment.	CTE is a central part of the work of the school. A variety of opportunities are available to students, ranging from dual enrollment in a local college to microcredentials in technical fields. There are sustained partnerships between local businesses, business organizations, and the school that deepen opportunities and help students build identities around new career possibilities.

that Geoff cowrote while he was working to integrate the best of business practices with the best educational leadership practices.[17] We encourage you to use this as an in-depth guide to identifying underlying causes of the difficulties that might emerge in a school and how to take a strategic approach that builds from a theory of action. It is a process that Geoff has led for teams of district leaders during a weeklong executive education session at Harvard Business School. For our purposes here, we suggest a slightly modified process focused on the strengths and challenges of rural schools. This approach involves six steps (shown in figure 8.2) that build from the comprehensive self-assessment we outlined in the first half of the chapter.

Step 1: Identify a Community Problem

Often in education there is a focus on school-specific reform. In our current era of test-based accountability, there can even be a

FIGURE 8.2   An improvement process for rural schools

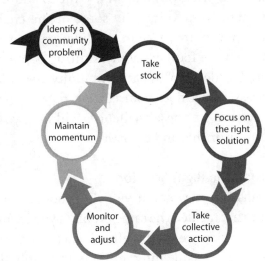

temptation to narrowly focus on problems identified in data, whether or not they are connected to larger underlying issues.[18] Rural schools are uniquely suited to address big challenges within a community because of their central role and the many services they deliver. Take time to look at the issues that emerged from your self-assessment. What are some of the big challenges that your school and community have the capacity to tackle? These could be anything from improving technology infrastructure to advancing career and technical education (CTE) to better supporting English language learners. When we lead schools through improvement processes, we always have an ear out for the issues that repeatedly come up and are within the school's sphere of influence. Ultimately, you want to identify a problem that you can substantially impact through the process you undertake in tackling it. Pick the problem that will help you build capacity and sustain change that positively impacts your students.

Step 2: Take Stock

Now that you know what problem you want to address, return to the self-assessment to help identify some of the challenges your school and community may face in tackling the issue at hand. Are there challenges in the local economy, shifting populations of students, or limited leadership? What community assets can you draw on in the process? What does your current data suggest about the problem? Being clear on these challenges will help you adapt your plan to what is reasonable and realistic.

Step 3: Focus on the Right Solution

In an ideal scenario, you would have a clear model of a community similar to yours that tackled the same problem you identified. There would be strong evidence of the effectiveness of their approach, and you could take the same interventions and apply them to your community with a good deal of confidence that you were using best practices. Unfortunately, rural populations are not commonly represented in educational research or case studies of best practices. That said, you can still research and evaluate potential solutions with an understanding that you may have to make adaptations for the solution to work in your school and community. Being clear on the weaknesses of existing tactics and how you expect to modify the new strategy will help you better understand where the change process is effective and where it requires further work.

Step 4: Take Collective Action

Rural schools are often tasked with delivery of multiple services in the small communities they represent, from medical and dental care at school to supplemental food programs in the summer.[19] The close networks of rural communities make it easier for school leaders to know the program leaders who operate beyond school walls.[20] This means that rural schools are uniquely equipped to invite many perspectives to the table to solve local problems.

Interorganizational collaboration can be an especially effective way to create impactful changes for children and families. Bringing diverse stakeholders together can help identify solutions that are better than what a school could design or deliver on its own. The challenge, of course, lies in creating an effective process. In *Improving Education Together*, Geoff partnered with Chad D'Entremont and Emily Kaur of the Rennie Center for Education Research and Policy to create a guide for how to lead this type of process.[21] The fundamental principle to keep in mind is to create one common and unifying goal, then work together toward that goal. One beautiful illustration of how multiple stakeholders can work together comes from Alberta, Canada, where the Alberta Family Wellness Initiative has taken on the struggle of addiction and mental health, particularly its impact on young children.[22] The collective has worked across schools, addiction treatment facilities, and health-care programs to promote healthy brain development and resilience in a number of different communities, including oil towns and Indigenous communities.

Once you have engaged your larger group with your problem and proposed solution, it's time to act. In any implementation process, you want to think about transparency and communication. Part of taking collective action is involving parents and students. Let them know what you are up to! Embrace their feedback and involve them in the process.

Step 5: Monitor and Adjust

To understand the impact of your strategy you will need an assessment plan. In *Making Assessment Matter*, Sky worked with Nonie Lesaux, a professor at the Harvard Graduate School of Education, on outlining the steps needed to create an assessment strategy based on a strategic purpose.[23] The book was the culmination of work done with many schools that were trying to improve reading skills, especially those with large numbers of ELLs. In situations where student populations do not neatly adhere to the guidelines usually followed in analyzing assessment results—such as rural and small schools—an assessment strategy is particularly important. The process described in the book focuses on using different types of measures over time to get a better sense of student outcomes that can be useful for driving instruction and making midcourse corrections when an intervention does not have the intended effect.

Step 6: Maintain Momentum

The problems that small and rural schools tackle can be overwhelming. The work can be daunting and even depressing. But when you lead a change process, you need to take care that the work gets carried through, even when urgent matters pop up and report cards are due. In order to maintain momentum, we recommend creating a project plan with a multiyear timeline. Periodic meetings to review the timeline will allow you to monitor progress. And, if you feel like your efforts are beginning to flag, count yourself in the company of others who have experienced bumps in the road to implementation.[24] Now is the time to begin the cycle again by going straight to the step on taking stock.

As you undertake an improvement process, be gentle on yourself and keep the big picture in mind. Ultimately, if the players involved deepen their skills and knowledge and you build connections and collaborations with other programs and schools, you will have undertaken the most important part of this work. The conditions that affect your school and learners have built over generations, and meaningful changes also take time and commitment. Improvement is like a muscle that is built with repeated use. As you more deeply identify problems and solutions, you will be increasingly better equipped to serve the unique people and needs of your own rural community.

9

Promises and Pitfalls of Serving Rural Education

WHAT KIND OF POLICIES are needed to support rural schools and educators? Throughout this book, we have kept an ongoing thread about the misalignment between educational reform and the reality and goals of rural life. We have mentioned approaches that try and push rural youth to move out to find professional opportunities in urban areas, whether or not that aligns with their aspirations or goals. We have noted education reform efforts that take a market-driven approach and explained why they do not work in rural areas without the population density required for programs like charter schools and vouchers. We have touched on the fact that testing is often unreliable in rural areas, where there are not enough children to make for clean statistical models. Across all of these elements of current educational reform that fail rural communities, perhaps the greatest is a centralized, top-down approach that hands down mandates from the federal and state level, without gaining input from rural communities or allowing for the accommodations that could make these approaches fit.[1] As we consider recommendations for policy and private philanthropy, we want to be clear that this centralized, top-down approach is one of the biggest challenges we face in creating a rural education system that promotes equality for all. This is particularly true given the tremendous diversity of rural communities.

Despite these clear and serious challenges, we have seen many initiatives that were successful for the rural communities they served. We have embraced work by Schafft, among others, that reminds us that schools are often at the heart of rural community development and can serve a central and vital role in building economic well-being and stability for families.[2] These are some of the questions we now face: How do we make our rural schools stronger more generally? What guidelines and processes can we offer in a climate where rural education has received little focus and attention? Where do we begin?

We are going to start this chapter with a cautionary tale. A few years ago, we heard some exciting news for our community and the schools our children attended. A nonprofit organization had been awarded a $30 million grant to improve cradle-to-career opportunities over five years in an area that included around ten thousand children under the age of eighteen. Our community and school district was among those targeted for the program. What a tremendous investment this represented! We could not wait to see what kinds of opportunities this new partnership might provide our children. We happily filled out the long questionnaire that was given to families so that the nonprofit grantee could better document its impact.

But as the year went on, we heard nothing else about this new program. At first we chalked it up to the initiative being new. We also knew the nonprofit was located outside the region and needed to establish relationships on the ground. But as the academic year turned to summer to a new academic year, we became curious about how this grant was being delivered. Now, to be clear, our home school district had done an excellent job partnering with other nonprofit organizations in the past. So, at the same time we were hearing nothing about a $6 million per year grant, we had learned about plenty of other programs. We knew all about a 21st Century Community Learning Centers grant that allowed wraparound care for students using a true enrichment model, providing services even in the summer and during snow days. We attended family literacy nights hosted by Save the Children and received a number of free books and school supplies from them and others. Our children ate the free breakfasts and lunches at school, and we received numerous pieces of information about where they could participate in summer feeding programs—among that "information" a pair of sunglasses that offered a number to text to find the closest meal. We got a special card from a local university that allowed schoolchildren and their families to attend any athletic game for free to help them get more familiar with college campuses. And our children even received free pairs of TOMS shoes and Bombas socks. There were additional programs we knew about but chose not to participate in: backpack programs that sent home food for the weekend, dental and pediatric care delivered at the school, an afterschool program for struggling readers, and a voluntary enrichment program that allowed children to learn more about the Bible, among many others.

How was it possible, with all of those supports and opportunities targeting schools and children in our struggling coal mining community, that we heard nothing about a $30 million grant? Not a single flyer, not a single informational brochure? When we asked teachers, why did they seem just as lost as we were? Instead of information, we found a large banner hanging in the elementary school gym that proclaimed the school as a partner of the nonprofit. Every morning as children congregated for announcements and the Pledge of Allegiance before being sent off to their homerooms, they sat beneath that banner. If this organization wanted to announce the grant in that way, why wasn't the program's work made visible to families?

Of course, it is possible that this nonprofit used the grant to make a tremendous impact on the children and/or educators it served, and we simply were not in the loop. But the next year the same nonprofit received another multimillion dollar grant to implement the same cradle-to-career services in a different Appalachian community. There, it was met with sharp criticism from the outset from that community's local leaders. You may wonder why that community challenged the nonprofit and its grant-supported plans.

As we mentioned, the nonprofit was located in a small city out-side of the distressed coal-producing communities it intended to serve with the millions of dollars in grant funds. The organization had become adept at identifying programs targeting Appalachia and securing the awards. But there were large gaps between the promises in the proposal and implementation on the ground. To some, it felt like the nonprofit had written the grant without ade-quately partnering with the local community and understanding its needs. The community that questioned the organization's plans had worked hard for many years to establish a local foundation to serve as a credible and professional steward of grant dollars spe-cifically to avoid a scenario where major grants were given to orga-nizations outside the region. Now people in the community were worried that this nonprofit would use the grant to hire people and pay overhead in the city it was located, and not in their rural com-munity, almost a two-hour drive away. If there was to be a major investment in cradle-to-career education, they wanted it to be owned and led locally. They were surprised by the announcement of the award and wanted to know: What was the plan? How had the grantee decided what was needed in their community? How would the nonprofit involve the local community in the process? What should the community expect as outcomes from this investment?

One major challenge facing historically marginalized rural communities is the struggle of self-determination, and this story explains how often we rely on outside organizations to serve rural communities without getting the results we want. This battle for self-determination is played out in the grant-making and grant-receiving processes. It is no surprise that having a critical mass of grant writers and administrators makes it far easier to identify potential grant opportunities, make a strong case, and receive grant dollars. And once a grant is received, that same administrative power makes it far easier to fulfill the reporting obligations of a grant. Small schools and nonprofits serving rural communities are far less likely to have this type of administrative machinery. In fact, this is one of the challenges for rural schools identified by the Department of Education.[3] It is also no surprise, then, that a theme that came up repeatedly as we researched this book is how often initiatives aimed at improving education for rural children are led by those we call "outsiders." These people may be familiar with evidence-based practices and have a ready and skilled staff, but they simply live elsewhere. Over and over again as we looked at programs for rural schools and communities, we saw this same trend—major grants to study and serve rural communities were being led by colleges and universities or other entities located in the least rural parts of a state or even the country.

As we close out this book, we want to bring voice to an experience that is rarely represented in literature on rural, marginalized communities, and that is the voice of the community members and practitioners who are the target of efforts to reduce inequality. In education, teachers unions have served the historic purpose of representing the practitioners. However, unions, which rely on the power of collectives and big numbers to have clout, do not have an easy job in rural America. And beyond teachers, there is an even greater void in representation from folks like us who are parents, practitioners, and community members. We believe firmly that many efforts aimed at our Appalachian community ultimately perpetuate poverty and inequality. We do not say this lightly, as we want nothing more than increased investment in our rural region and others. However, we find that very little of the money intended to support our community actually finds its way here. Meanwhile, the real work of rural education continues on the ground, led by local people who are doing the best work they can with the resources at hand. Rarely are they acknowledged as experts, and even more rarely are their needs met. Instead, public and private dollars are often funneled into the most urban parts of the state to create staff positions and pay outside consultants and experts. In the end, there is very little to show for the work that they do.

If we are to consider policy implications for rural education, we must do so carefully and with clear eyes. Over and again research shows that what makes any reform effort work is the quality of implementation, and the quality of implementation is driven by relationships. There is no shortcut to rural America, no fast pass that allows you to get there quickly and create the deep networks that are needed for successful implementation. Because those administering grants often live elsewhere, a significant amount of their implementation time involves driving (or flying) to the community. This typically means they are in the rural community briefly and are not able to form deep relationships. So while we agree wholeheartedly that education in rural America requires greater investment, we also believe that this investment needs to be strategic and carefully delivered to the rural communities.

The efficiencies of scale that a large university has may make this seem like a wise approach. However, without the deep relationships that are built when you are embedded in a community, programs tend to be piecemeal and do not build local capacity. Poverty persists and educational attainment remains low. And local people become wary and disillusioned after they hear about many big approaches, grants, and ideas, but see little traction on the ground. Or, worse, they become frustrated when they work very hard to make improvements, only to see large programs come through and take the credit for their progress. If we are going to use education to help rural America during a time of economic transition, we simply cannot afford to fund $30 million initiatives that do not have a clear and compelling impact in the communities they serve. Let's take a look at a typical model for improving rural education and the associated pitfalls it represents.

A TYPICAL EXPERIENCE AND ASSOCIATED PITFALLS

What is it like to participate in big initiatives aimed at improving rural communities? In our experience, there is a typical model that is implemented again and again by the outside university. The grantee receives money to convene stakeholders. At these meetings, the grantee provides professional development and leads an action planning exercise. The rural practitioners are then charged with implementing their learning on the ground.

One example is a meeting that Sky went to when she was running Little School, an early childhood program in a remote part of Harlan County. The meeting was led by a nonprofit called to bring together early education and care providers in a five-county area that is part of a federal promise zone comprising counties that have been sharply and directly impacted by the decline in coal jobs and have some of the highest rates of social distress. Sky drove two and a half hours, one way, to the meeting, which was held outside of the five-county region. The meeting took place in a conference room of a beautiful hotel in the city where the nonprofit was headquartered. A decadent breakfast and lunch were served, and the room was filled with well over fifty people, each receiving their name badges and binders. The morning was spent overviewing data on young children in the region, and it was grim indeed: child poverty, teen pregnancies, and kindergarten readiness rates were hung up on the wall to analyze and dissect. All of these data pointed to some real challenges that practitioners in the coal-impacted communities would face in serving young children. Everyone in the room agreed that the need to serve young children in these communities was overwhelming.

After lunch the meeting progressed to action steps and participants were instructed to break up by tables into the communities they served. This was the moment where the difficulties of leading change efforts from the outside begin to emerge. Of the fifty or so people in the room, around ten lived in and worked in the rural counties that were the focus of the meeting. Everyone else in the room was a technical assistance provider, consultant, or administrator who lived outside the service region. Entire counties were unrepresented. Sky found herself at a table with two preschool teachers from her county; the three of them were charged with creating an early childhood working group that would bring together the important players of their county for regular meetings to build collaboration. The problem was that the three of them represented one nonprofit and the preschool program of one elementary school. There was nobody at the table from the other five elementary schools, or the school district office, or Head Start, or Early Intervention, not to mention home-based providers or the one private parochial school that offered preschool and day care services.

Sky and the two preschool teachers were tasked with identifying these leaders in early childhood and bringing them together for a monthly meeting. But as they worked to hammer out logistics, a number of challenges emerged. The leading organization did not know the names or contact information of the leaders they wanted to include. Then it became clear that there was no budget to do this work. They were told there was no money for facilities or meals. There was no stipend for the people on the ground doing the work of inviting people and scheduling and hosting. Instead, the outside organization spearheading the efforts offered a trained facilitator who could attend the meeting and facilitate the conversation. This service was offered for free.

During a break, Sky visited a table that represented a neighboring county. There she found a larger group, but they were facing their own issues with the afternoon's activity. It happened that this community had already established an early childhood working group. When they made the long drive to the meeting they had no idea that this organization was bringing them together to duplicate their efforts. They were similarly surprised that the grant convened various stakeholder groups but did not offer any money to back the work on the ground. What they had hoped for was funding for a staff person in their community who could do the work of bridging the various programs for staff trainings and for families that were seeking education and care options. They did not see the value-add of a free outside facilitator.

For the closing activity, the local early childhood practitioners were to make measurable commitments of what they would achieve to advance the goals of the grant. Each was supposed to stand and make a pledge of how they would get the work done. You could sense the unease of the local childcare providers, who were supposed to take on considerable extra work beyond their current duties. In contrast, the day was considered a major success by those who received the grant. Had they not convened five counties and come away with commitments to establish early childhood working groups in each? Isn't it important to bring together a variety of community stakeholders?

Let's talk about some common pitfalls represented by this situation and why work in rural communities may not gain the traction we are hoping—even when the work accomplished looks good on paper.

- ### Pitfall 1: Led by outsiders
In this case, an initiative for five rural Appalachian counties was led by an organization located at least an hour's drive from the closest location, in an urban center. And while there is nothing wrong in

forging urban and rural partnerships, this approach can have major downfalls, as illustrated here. The leaders of the hosting organization were not able to get the important players at the table. They were not even sure who should be invited, and instead cast a net to see who they could get and then charged the participants with the actual work of creating the network. This lack of connection led to real difficulties when implementing a network intended to bring diverse stakeholders together for common goals. Their unfamiliarity with the work being done on the ground resulted in duplication of effort in one community, and in others the work simply never got off the ground. When Sky reached out for resources—such as information on childcare vouchers—the nonprofit was unable to provide answers to the questions that arose. Imagine how different this scenario would have been if it had been led by local folks who were deeply familiar with the services currently offered and with the leaders of all the early childhood organizations.

- *Pitfall 2: Expertise is top-down*

This day of development followed a classic model in educational professional development. One organization served as the experts for the day. They brought in practitioners from rural communities and showed them the data on their own community. The leaders of the event then had participants go through an exercise that explained the action steps they should take for their communities. Imagine flipping this common scenario around. What if the people who held the workshop had, instead, sought out the expertise of the practitioners? What if they asked them to bring their own challenges and successes and share what had worked for them? What if they had asked the participants to come up with a plan that would provide the support and resources they needed? Of course, a mix of these two approaches might be the strongest one. But all too often, those who are on the ground solving problems are not asked to share their successes or needs.

- *Pitfall 3: Limited local investment*

Creating paid leadership positions for local people—and allowing them to remain in their rural communities to do their work—is one major way that we invest in a community through grant dollars. But if we look at how funds were disbursed for this particular meeting, we see that the reinvestment in the rural counties was almost nil. The facilitators and technical assistance providers live elsewhere and pay taxes in other communities. Payment for the meal and facility went to the small city where the workshop was held. We understand the urge to hold meetings in cities with greater amenities and easier access. By definition, rural communities are hard to get to, and it may take more effort to find venues located within the community. But at the same time, we believe it is critical to situate the work in the communities where it will be done. Even beyond dollars, we invest in a community when we allow the people of that community to serve as leaders. We have seen over and again that the initiatives that have the most teeth on the ground have the highest proportional reinvestment in the local community.

- *Pitfall 4: Convening without follow-through*

Building strong connections between new and existing programs is an important part of meaningful work. In rural areas, it can be difficult for practitioners to gather and partner because of real difficulties around geographic distance. This is one reason why a "convener" model is very popular in successful grant applications for rural communities. The host organization convenes the stakeholders, guides them through a strategic process, and then sends them off to do the work. But education reform works best when efforts are sustained over time in close partnership. Periodic meetings do not allow for the deep collaborative processes that build coalitions among stakeholders and across schools and school leaders, unless there is clear and sustained follow-through.

A RURAL-CENTERED APPROACH

So how should we be investing our money to better support rural communities? When we see successful programs, they share many of the same traits. They are centered in the communities that they are trying to serve. The programs are led by people who live in the rural community. They build capacity on the ground and strengthen connections between rural schools and rural areas so that they can share resources and problem-solve together. They expand opportunities by bringing in outside expertise, but only as an additive to a foundation solidly built in the community being served. Money is spent to make improvements to the rural community. Ultimately, such programs represent a true investment in the rural community.

We believe adopting the following five guidelines will support the work already under way in rural schools across America:

1. Treat rural school development as community and leadership development
2. Invest in infrastructure, particularly broadband, to increase rural school opportunities
3. Build coalitions, connections, and networks
4. Integrate education with economic growth
5. Prioritize rural schools and communities

We believe it is critical that policy makers, educational leaders, and private philanthropies adopt this approach if they are to serve rural schools.

Step 1: Treat Rural School Development as Community and Leadership Development

Rural schools play a deeply embedded, central role in their communities, and the best policy approaches focus on community development.[4] We believe that one of the best ways to build a rural community is to invest in local leadership capacity. For example, in Grand Rapids, Minnesota, one of the greatest successes of Invest Early was how the organization took young mothers and set them on a leadership pipeline through increasing professional opportunities and training in education.[5] We have seen this same kind of approach work for the Kentucky Valley Education Cooperative, where local teachers are the ones presenting best practices and new ideas. In fact, viewing the local community as a source of knowledge and expertise is a pedagogical tool that has been central to many educational movements that have been led by educators.[6]

A large part of community and leadership development is creating structures that require rural educators to serve in leadership roles. For example, the intention of Oregon's House Bill 4051 was to create a Task Force on Rural Education.[7] The initial focus was on evaluating and providing recommendations for some of the biggest challenges facing rural schools in the state. These included graduation rates, student mobility, serving underrepresented students, and advancing postsecondary education. But rather than just create the task force, the bill spelled out specifically what experiences and roles the fourteen task members must represent. Along with district leadership, the bill required that the task force include, for example, a special education teacher and a teacher who works with English language learners. This approach formalized rural representation and will allow rural voices to continue to inform decisions even when the state sees changes in political leadership. This type of action is key to adequately serving rural schools and should be a model for other states.

Step 2: Invest in Infrastructure, Particularly Broadband, to Expand Opportunities

The reality is that rural K–12 districts have limited resources, particularly technology and other tools needed to help students access opportunities beyond what is offered in the school itself. This might include dual enrollment in classes and online technical training that would allow better preparation for postsecondary enrollment and skilled trades in technology. As long as there are large gaps in access to high-speed internet, rural schools will be left out of one of the key strategies that could level the playing field. For example, online and blended learning such as Kahn Academy, Microsoft's TEAL program, and Project Lead the Way are all initiatives that should expand opportunities for rural students. But, without adequate internet, these and other online programs will never reach their full potential.

Wisconsin has made a specific investment in rural information technology infrastructure through grants designed to provide technological support and infrastructure to classrooms and libraries.[8] The intention is to establish high-speed internet connections needed to improve the connectivity and instructional capacity of classrooms in rural school districts. The competitiveness of the grant is explicitly based on the percentage of students receiving free and reduced-price lunch. The grant application process is simplified so that any teacher or librarian can help improve digital access in their school.

Step 3: Build Coalitions, Connections, and Networks

As we looked at programs that have built increased STEM and career opportunities for students, we saw an emphasis on collaborative arrangements between schools. This type of resource sharing is vital to rural schools that do not have the staff or budget to fulfill their own needs. If we look broadly, we can see that many successful initiatives focus on building connections between practitioners, and particularly between school leaders.

But perhaps the very best approaches to rural education go beyond the school walls to build broader coalitions for change. After all, sustained improvement requires the involvement of all stakeholders, particularly parents and teachers. *Leveling the Playing Field for Rural Students*, compiled by the School Superintendents

Association and the Rural School and Community Trust, provides policy recommendations for legislators.[9] This report emphasizes again and again the crucial involvement of all stakeholders in a rural community, including health care providers and local business owners. It is this type of integrated approach that will help solve the bigger issues in rural education.

Step 4: Integrate Education with Economic Growth

At a time when rural education is often seen as a way to educate youth *away* from their community rather than *for* their community, the importance of situating education in the economic growth of a community is critical.[10] One promising approach is South Carolina's implementation of the Workforce Innovation and Opportunity Act, a federal program that helps job seekers access education, employment, training, and support services, and also helps fund Apprenticeship Carolina, a program run out of the South Carolina Technical College System that assists local employers in setting up training and apprenticeship programs.[11] This act promotes partnerships that connect businesses with high schools and technical colleges to collaborate on internships and dual credit and certificate programs for students—especially in rural areas—interested in skilled trades. The program includes Workforce Innovation Grants that promote these partnerships. Recent grant awards highlight the many players involved in this type of work, including community and technical colleges, school districts, alternative programs for out-of-school youth, and programs serving youth and adults with disabilities.[12]

Step 5: Prioritize Rural Schools and Communities

We add our voices to the many who argue that rural schools and communities must be a funding priority.[13] However, to make such efforts succeed we need to streamline the processes that make understaffed rural and small schools struggle to secure and administer grants.[14] For example, the Strengthening Career and Technical Education for the 21st Century Act is a federal law that seeks to simplify the application process for career and technical education grants.[15]

We may also need to focus on distributing opportunities across multiple different organizations. For example, the Appalachian Regional Commission administers POWER (Partnerships for Opportunity and Workforce and Economic Revitalization) grants to help promote educational and workforce initiatives in communities that have experienced job losses due to the decline of the coal industry. This organization has funded important work, but it began to realize that the same groups were receiving grants again and again. In 2018, it implemented a new rule: organizations could apply for and serve as the fiscal sponsors for only one grant at a time.[16] We witnessed how this change shook things up on the ground. Suddenly, everyone was looking for new partners. Organizations that had never previously been included in discussions of grants were suddenly taking leadership roles. This simple change made the process accessible to a greater range of applicants.

We also need to be aware of how we use data to drive change in our rural schools. We believe that reliable performance data is crucial to guiding our efforts and evaluating impact. At the same time, rural communities face challenges that make it clear that data on its own it is not enough. Rather than seeking explicit outcomes, we may need to use data to carefully follow specific cases and narratives. Data should be used in a benchmarking capacity with multiple measures over time so that it becomes a tool to inform work.

A FUTURE FOR RURAL EDUCATION

Is there a future in a modern, globalized world for rural America? Will rural and urban areas become increasingly divided and separated? Can small, rural communities build the leadership and capacity needed to take charge of their own problems? These are some of the big questions in the conversation on rural schooling in America. In this book, we have taken a different stance. We argue that rural communities are diverse and face all different kinds of circumstances. We believe that rural life has value and that supporting rural communities should not involve pressuring individuals to move to access career opportunities. Instead, rural education should be seen as a way to build rural communities into thriving places that create opportunity—including the opportunity to stay or go.

But maybe rural America is more than just a viable place to live. We would argue that many of the struggles of rural America forecast what is to come more broadly in the country, particularly in the ongoing struggle to have a socially just and equal society. If you consider some of the biggest challenges of our time, you realize that these struggles are playing out in rural America. Take, for instance, global climate change. There is often a perception that sophisticated urban Americans are the ones who embrace the science of global climate change, but it is rural Americans who are living it out daily. You can go to any grandma in the mountains and she can tell you very clearly how planting, hunting, and harvesting have all changed greatly from the patterns that she knew from her childhood; indeed, the patterns and traditions that had been handed down through generations. Witness terrible flooding in America's dairylands in the Midwest, or fires ravaging California, and you will see rural people on the forefront of the catastrophes of our time—and dealing with them in an era where the budget will not be able to stretch to accommodate all needs. As we write this book, America has forty million people who have suddenly lost their jobs because of the coronavirus pandemic. We are seeing at scale the kind of economic bust that rural America has already had to absorb. As big machines plow up fields the size of a football field in minutes, replacing work that once took hundreds of hands, you can see the pain points that later hit when people could no longer gather or shop. When you suddenly consider replacing the income of every Uber driver, you see an economic challenge that rural America has already wrestled with. Rural America is a case test for the near horizon, the proverbial canary in the coal mine.

But not only is rural America a test case for problems that are on the verge of our times, it is also on the forefront of positive changes. A connection to place and history and deep social ties are increasingly part of a collective yearning in a country where, overall, more people value family relationships over wealth.[17] Simple living, connection with nature, and deep ties are all strengths that rural America brings to our society. Rural Americans are the ones who understand how food got to your table and paper into your hands. This is valuable knowledge.

As we think about these big issues, we have to keep in mind that where challenges hit families, they hit schools. We see this with our own children, whose school provides the prism that allows us to see the many issues children all over America face today. If we had a dream for rural education, it would be this—that a rural life is something people embrace, accepted as one of the many ways people choose to exist in a country that was founded on personal liberty. And that, one day, our country is seen as a place of opportunity for all neighborhoods, regardless of social class, race, and whether the view out your window is wide open plains or high city towers.

NOTES

Introduction

1. Stacey Childress and Geoff Marietta, *A Problem-Solving Approach to Designing and Implementing a Strategy to Improve Performance* (Cambridge, MA: Harvard University Public Education Leadership Project, 2008), http://pelp.fas.harvard.edu/files/hbs-test/files/pel056p2.pdf; Geoff Marietta, Chad D'Entremont, and Emily Murphy Kaur, *Improving Education Together* (Cambridge, MA: Harvard Education Press, 2017).
2. Nonie Lesaux, Emily Phillips Galloway, and Sky Marietta, *Teaching Advanced Literacy Skills: A Guide for Leaders in Linguistically Diverse Schools* (New York: Guilford Press, 2016).
3. You can learn more about Pine Mountain Settlement School and our work there in the article "City on a Hill" by Alexander Gelfand for the Harvard Business School Alumni Bulletin, www.alumni.hbs.edu/stories/Pages/story-impact.aspx?num=7034&sf103844897=1.
4. "Strengthening the Rural Economy," US Council of Economic Advisors, https://obamawhitehouse.archives.gov/administration/eop/cea/factsheets-reports/strengthening-the-rural-economy/introduction; "Rural Educational Attainment Has Been Rising," US Department of Agriculture, https://www.ers.usda.gov/data-products/chart-gallery/gallery/chart-detail/?chartId=76841.
5. Gary D. Funk, "Rural School Snub: The Inequity of Title I Funding," *Chicago Policy Review*, 2012, http://chicagopolicyreview.org/2012/02/13/rural-school-snub-the-inequity-of-title-i-funding; Cynthia M. Duncan, "Community Development in Rural America: Collaborative, Re-gional, and Comprehensive," Investing in What Works for America's Communities, http://www.whatworksforamerica.org/ideas/community-development-in-rural-america-collaborative-regional-and-comprehensive.
6. "State and County Quickfacts," US Census Bureau, http://quickfacts.census.gov.

7. Harvard University Opportunity Insights, "Opportunity Atlas," https://www.opportunityatlas.org.

Chapter 1

1. Michael Ratcliffe, "A Century of Delineating a Changing Landscape: The Census Bureau's Urban and Rural Classification, 1910 to 2010" (paper presented at the annual meeting of the Social Science History Association, Baltimore, MD, November 14, 2015); Louise Reynnells and Patricia La Caille John, "What Is Rural?," Rural Information Center, US Department of Agriculture, 2016, https://files.eric.ed.gov/fulltext/ED565858.pdf; Craig Howley, Paul Theobald, and Aimee Howley, "What Rural Education Research Is of Most Worth? A Reply to Arnold, Newman, Gaddy, and Dean," Journal of Research in Rural Education 20, no. 18 (2005): 1; Catharine Biddle and Amy Price Azano, "Constructing and Reconstructing the 'Rural School Problem': A Century of Rural Education Research," Review of Research in Education 40, no. 1 (2016): 298–325, doi:10.3102/0091732x16667700.
2. Leonard Cohen, "Anthem," Columbia, track 5 on The Future, 1992.
3. "Population: 1790–1990," Population and Housing Unit Counts, US Census Bureau, https://www.census.gov/population/censusdata/table-4.pdf.
4. "New Census Data Show Differences Between Urban and Rural Populations," American Community Survey: 2011–2015, US Census Bureau, December 8, 2016, https://www.census.gov/newsroom/press-releases/2016/cb16-210.html.
5. "New Census Data Show"; "Population: 1790–1990."
6. John Cromartie, "Rural America at a Glance: 2018 Edition," Economic Information Bulletin 2018, US Department of Agriculture, https://www.ers.usda.gov/webdocs/publications/90556/eib-200.pdf.
7. Eduardo Porter, "The Hard Truths of Trying to 'Save' the Rural Economy," New York Times, December 14, 2018, https://www.nytimes.com/interactive/2018/12/14/opinion/rural-america-trump-decline.html; Paul Krugman, "Getting Real About Rural America," New York Times, March 18, 2019, https://www.nytimes.com/2019/03/18/opinion/rural-america-economic-decline.html.
8. Peter Lattman, "The Origins of Justice Stewart's 'I know It When I See It'," Law Blog, Wall Street Journal, September 27, 2007, https://blogs.wsj.com/law/2007/09/27/the-origins-of-justice-stewarts-i-know-it-when-i-see-it.
9. Biddle and Azano, "Constructing and Reconstructing."
10. Michael Ratcliffe et al., Defining Rural at the US Census Bureau, 2016, https://www2.census.gov/geo/pdfs/reference/ua/Defining_Rural.pdf.
11. Ratcliffe, "A Century of Delineating."
12. Ratcliffe.
13. Reynnells and John, "What Is Rural?"
14. "USDA Income and Property Eligibility Site," US Department of Agriculture, Rural

Development, http://eligibility.sc.egov.usda.gov/eligibility/welcomeAction.do.

15. "Rural Veterans," US Department of Veterans Affairs, Office of Rural Health, https://www.ruralhealth.va.gov/aboutus/ruralvets.asp.

16. "Rural Education in America," National Center for Education Statistics, Institute of Education Science, https://nces.ed.gov/surveys/ruraled/Definitions.asp.

17. Howley, Theobald, and Howley, "What Rural Education Research."

18. Howley, Theobald, and Howley; Biddle and Azano, "Constructing and Reconstructing"; Mara Casey Tieken, Why Rural Schools Matter (Chapel Hill: University of North Carolina Press, 2014.)

19. Tieken, 5.

20. Ratcliffe et al., Defining Rural; Reynnells and John, "What Is Rural?"

21. Megan Lavalley, Out of the Loop (Alexandria, VA: Center for Public Education, 2018), https://cdn-files.nsba.org/s3fs-public/10901-5071_CPE_Rural_School_Report_Web_FINAL.pdf.

22. Danielle Kurtzleben, "Rural Voters Played a Big Part in Helping Trump Defeat Clinton," NPR, November 14, 2016, https://www.npr.org/2016/11/14/501737150/rural-voters-played-a-big-part-in-helping-trump-defeat-clinton.

23. Jagdish Sheth and Rajendra Sisodia, Tectonic Shift: The Geoeconomic Realignment of Globalizing Markets (Thousand Oaks, CA: Sage Publications, 2006).

24. "Strengthening the Rural Economy: The Current State of Rural America," US Council of Economic Advisors, 2014, https://obamawhitehouse.archives .gov/administration/eop/cea/factsheets-reports/ strengthening-the-rural-economy/the-current-state-of-rural-america.

25. Brian Thiede et al., "The Divide Between Rural and Urban America, in 6 Charts," US News & World Report, March 20, 2017, https://www.usnews.com/ news/national-news/articles/2017-03-20/6-charts-that-illustrate-the-divide-between-rural-and-urban-america.

26. Brian Thiede, Hyojung Kim, and Matthew Valasik, "Concentrated Poverty Increased in Both Rural and Urban Areas Since 2000, Reversing Declines in the 1990s," Carsey Research National Issue Brief 129, Carsey School of Public Policy, University of New Hampshire, fall 2017, https://scholars.unh.edu/cgi/ viewcontent.cgi?article=1324&context=carsey; Reid Wilson, "Rural Poverty Skyrockets as Jobs Move Away," The Hill, December 05, 2017, https://thehill .com/homenews/state-watch/363415-rural-poverty-skyrockets-as-jobs-move-away; "Rural Employment and Unemployment," US Department of Agriculture, Economic Research Service, https://www.ers.usda.gov/topics/rural-economy-population/employment-education/rural-employment-and-unemployment.

27. Edward L. Glaeser, ed., Agglomeration Economics (Chicago: University of Chicago Press, 2010), http://www.nber.org/books/glae08-1; Enrico Moretti, The New Geography of Jobs (Boston: Houghton Mifflin Harcourt, 2012); "Rural Employment and Unemployment."

28. Claudia Goldin and Lawrence Katz, *The Race Between Education and Technology* (Cambridge, MA: Belknap Press, 2008).

29. Ralph Heimlich and William Anderson, *Development at the Urban Fringe and Beyond: Impacts on Agriculture and Rural Land*, Agricultural Economic Report No. 803, US Department of Agriculture, 2001; Tim Walker, "Many Rural Students Still 'Invisible' to Lawmakers," *NEA Today*, November 26, 2019, http://neatoday.org/2019/11/26/many-rural-students-still-invisible-to-lawmakers.

30. Gary Funk, "Rural School Snub: The Inequity of Title I Funding," *Chicago Policy Review*, February 13, 2012, http://chicagopolicyreview.org/2012/02/13/rural-school-snub-the-inequity-of-title-i-funding.

31. Lauren Camera and Lindsey Cook, "Title I: Rich School Districts Get Millions Meant for Poor Kids," *US News & World Report*, June 1, 2016, https://www.usnews.com/news/articles/2016-06-01/title-i-rich-school-districts-get-millions-in-federal-money-meant-for-poor-kids; Jennifer Cohen Kabaker, "A Closer Look at Title I Funding in Urban Versus Rural Districts," *New America*, Federal Education Budget Project Blog, February 27, 2012, https://www.newamerica.org/education-policy/federal-education-budget-project/ed-money-watch/a-closer-look-at-title-i-funding-in-urban-versus-rural-districts.

32. Kabaker, "A Closer Look at Title I"; Funk, "Rural School Snub."

33. All Children Are Equal Act, H.R. 2485, 112th Congress (2011–2012), July 11, 2011, https://www.congress.gov/bill/112th-congress/house-bill/2485.

34. "Small Rural School Achievement Program," Title V of the Elementary and Secondary Education Act of 1965, US Department of Education, https://www2.ed.gov/programs/reapsrsa/legislation.html.

35. Daniel Showalter, Robert Klein, Jerry Johnson, and Sara Hartman, *Why Rural Matters 2015–2016: Understanding the Changing Landscape* (Washington, DC: Rural School and Community Trust, June 2017).

36. "The Facts on Rural Schools," Public Schools First NC, March 3, 2020, https://www.publicschoolsfirstnc.org/resources/fact-sheets/the-facts-on-rural-schools.

37. Rick Cohen and John Barkhamer, *Beyond City Limits: The Philanthropic Needs of Rural America* (Washington, DC: National Committee for Responsive Philanthropy, 2004).

38. *Giving USA 2019: The Annual Report on Philanthropy for the Year 2018* (Chicago: Giving USA Foundation, 2019).

39. John Pender, *Foundation Grants to Rural Areas from 2005 to 2010: Trends and Patterns*, Economic Information Bulletin 141, Economic Research Service, US Department of Agriculture, June 2015; Tim Marema, "Rural Gets Less Foundation Money," *Daily Yonder*, June 29, 2015, https://www.dailyyonder.com/rural-gets-less-foundation-money/2015/06/29.

40. Pender, *Foundation Grants.*

41. Ryan Schlegel and Stephanie Pang, *As the South Grows: Strong Roots* (Washington,

DC: National Committee for Responsible Philanthropy, 2017), https://www
.ncrp.org/publication/as-the-south-grows-strong-roots.

42. "Our Issues," Rebuild Rural, https://rebuildrural.com/#page2.

43. "Our Issues."

44. Rural Health Information Hub, "Social Determinants of Health for Rural
People," 2020 https://www.ruralhealthinfo.org/topics/social-determinants-
of-health

45. Douglas Blanks Hindman, "The Rural-Urban Digital Divide," *Journalism and
Mass Communication Quarterly* 77, no. 3 (2000): 549–60.

46. Hindman.

47. Defined as 25 megabits per second (Mbps) up/3 Mbps down.

48. Blair Levin and Carol Mattey, "In Infrastructure Plan, a Big Opening for
Rural Broadband," Brookings, February 13, 2017, https://www.brookings.edu/
blog/the-avenue/2017/02/13/in-infrastructure-plan-a-big-opening-for-rural-
broadband.

49. Monica Anderson, "About a Quarter of Rural Americans Say Access to High-
Speed Internet Is a Major Problem," Pew Research Center, Fact Tank, September
20, 2018, https://www.pewresearch.org/fact-tank/2018/09/10/about-a-quarter-
of-rural-americans-say-access-to-high-speed-internet-is-a-major-problem.

50. Allison Suttle, "Rural America Faces a Healthcare Access Crisis," *Modern
Healthcare*, September 21, 2019, https://www.modernhealthcare.com/opinion-
editorial/rural-america-faces-healthcare-access-crisis.

51. Nicole Fisher, "Urbanization Leaves Rural America in a Health Care Crisis,"
Forbes, October 25, 2019, https://www.forbes.com/sites/nicolefisher/2019/10/25/
urbanization-leaves-rural-america-in-a-health-care-crisis/#684678d91b2a.

52. "About the American Community Survey," US Census Bureau, https://www
.census.gov/programs-surveys/acs/about.html.

53. Janice Probst et al., "Current State of Child Health in Rural America: How
Context Shapes Children's Health," *Journal of Rural Health* 34, no. 1 (February
2018): s3–s12, doi:10.1111/jrh.12222s.

54. Gopal Singh et al., "All-Cause and Cause-Specific Mortality Among US Youth:
Socioeconomic and Rural-Urban Disparities and International Patterns," *Journal of Urban Health* 90, no. 3 (2013): 388–405, doi:10.1007/s11524-012-9744-0.

55. "A Shifting Epidemic: Rural Areas Were Ground Zero of Opioid Crisis, But
Cities Now Outpace Those Death Rates," *Kaiser Health News*, August 2, 2019,
https://khn.org/morning-breakout/a-shifting-epidemic-rural-areas-were-ground-
zero-of-opioid-crisis-but-cities-now-outpace-those-death-rates.

56. "How Much Does Opioid Treatment Cost?," *Medications to Treat Opioid Use Disorder*, National Institute of Drug Abuse, June 2018, https://www.drugabuse
.gov/publications/research-reports/medications-to-treat-opioid-addiction/
how-much-does-opioid-treatment-cost.

57. Opportunity Atlas, http://www.opportunityatlas.org.

58. *Leveling the Playing Field for Rural Students*, AASA, The School Superintendent's Association, November 2017, https://www.aasa.org/uploadedFiles/Policy_and_Advocacy/Resources/AASA_Rural_Equity_Report_FINAL.pdf.

59. Alan Flippen, "Where Are the Hardest Places to Live in the US?," *New York Times*, June 26, 2014, https://www.nytimes.com/2014/06/26/upshot/where-are-the-hardest-places-to-live-in-the-us.html.

60. "Where Americans Find Meaning in Life," Pew Research Center, November 20, 2018, https://www.pewforum.org/2018/11/20/where-americans-find-meaning-in-life.

61. Allison Flemming et al., "Resilience and Strength of Rural Communities," in Disability and Vocational Rehabilitation in Rural Settings, ed. Debra Harley et al. (Cham, Switzerland: Springer, 2018), 117–36, https://link.springer.com/chapter/10.1007/978-3-319-64786-9_7.

Chapter 2

1. Janet Adamy and Paul Overberg, "Rural America Is the New 'Inner City,'" *Wall Street Journal*, May 26, 2017, https://www.wsj.com/articles/rural-america-is-the-new-inner-city-1495817008.

2. Eduardo Porter, "The Hard Truths of Trying to 'Save' the Rural Economy," *New York Times*, December 14, 2018, https://www.nytimes.com/interactive/2018/12/14/opinion/rural-america-trump-decline.html.

3. "What Percentage of Americans Currently Live in the Town or City Where They Grew Up?," North American Moving Services, https://www.northamerican.com/infographics/where-they-grew-up.

4. "Where Americans Find Meaning in Life," Pew Research Center, November 20, 2018, https://www.pewforum.org/2018/11/20/where-americans-find-meaning-in-life.

5. Quoctrung Bui and Claire Cain Miller, "The Typical American Lives Only 18 Miles from Mom," *New York Times*, December 23, 2015, https://www.nytimes.com/interactive/2015/12/24/upshot/24up-family.html.

6. "Where Americans Find Meaning"; "What Percentage of Americans."

7. Bui and Miller, "The Typical American."

8. Raj Chetty and Nathaniel Hendren, "The Impacts of Neighborhoods on Intergenerational Mobility II: County-Level Estimates," *Quarterly Journal of Economics* 133, no. 3 (2018): 1163–228, doi:10.1093/qje/qjy006; Nadarajan Chetty et al., "Where Is the Land of Opportunity? The Geography of Intergenerational Mobility in the United States," *Quarterly Journal of Economics* 129, no. 4 (2014): 1553, doi:10.1093/qje/qju022; Eleanor Krause and Richard V. Reeves, "Rural Dreams: Upward Mobility in America's Countryside," Center on Children and Families at Brookings, September 2017, https://www.brookings.edu/

wp-content/uploads/2017/08/es_20170905_ruralmobility.pdf.

9. Chetty and Hendren, "The Impacts of Neighborhoods"; Chetty et al., "Where Is the Land"; Reeves, "Rural Dreams."

10. Reeves, "Rural Dreams."

11. Bruce A. Weber et al., "Upward Mobility of Low-Income Youth in Metropolitan, Micropolitan, and Rural America," ANNALS of the American Academy of Political and Social Science 672, no. 1 (2017): 103–22, doi:10.1177/0002716217713477; Bruce A. Weber et al., "Intergenerational Mobility of Low-Income Youth in Metropolitan and Non-metropolitan America: A Spatial Analysis," Regional Science Policy & Practice 10, no. 2 (2018): 87–101, doi:10.1111/rsp3.12122.

12. Alemayehu Bishaw and Kirby G. Posey, "A Comparison of Rural and Urban America: Household Income and Poverty," US Census Bureau, December 8, 2016, https://www.census.gov/newsroom/blogs/random-samplings/2016/12/a_comparison_of_rura.html.

13. Christopher Mazur, "Rural Residents More Likely to Own Homes Than Urban Residents," US Census Bureau, September 27, 2017, https://www.census.gov/library/stories/2017/09/rural-home-ownership.html.

14. Chartis Center for Rural Health, "The Rural Health Safety Net Under Pressure: Rural Hospital Vulnerability," February 2020, https://www.ivantageindex.com/wp-content/uploads/2020/02/CCRH_Vulnerability-Research_FiNAL-02.14.20.pdf.

15. Danielle Farrie, Robert Kim, and David G. Sciarra, "Making the Grade 2019: How Fair Is School Funding in Your State?," Education Law Center, 2019, https://edlawcenter.org/assets/Making-the-Grade/Making%20the%20Grade%202019.pdf.

16. Erica Frankenberg et al., "Harming Our Common Future: America's Segregated Schools 65 Years After Brown," Civil Rights Project and Center for Education and Civil Rights, 2019, https://www.civilrightsproject.ucla.edu/research/k-12-education/integration-and-diversity/harming-our-common-future-americas-segregated-schools-65-years-after-brown/Brown-65-050919v4-final.pdf.

17. Frankenberg et al.

18. Mara Casey Tieken, "The Spatialization of Racial Inequity and Educational Opportunity: Rethinking the Rural/Urban Divide," Peabody Journal of Education 92, no. 3 (2017): 385–404, doi:10.1080/0161956X.2017.1324662.

19. Frankenberg et al., "Harming Our Common Future."

20. David Card and Jesse Rothstein, "Racial Segregation and the Black–White Test Score Gap," Journal of Public Economics 91, no. 11–12 (2007): 2158–84, doi:10.1016/j.jpubeco.2007.03.006; Robert Balfanz and Nettie Legters, Locating the Dropout Crisis: Which High Schools Produce the Nation's Dropouts? Where Are They Located? Who Attends Them?, Report No. 70 (Baltimore, MD: Johns Hopkins University, Center for Research on the Education of Students Placed at Risk, 2004).

21. Scott Page, The Difference: How the Power of Diversity Creates Better Groups, Firms,

Schools, and Societies, new ed. (Princeton, NJ: Princeton University Press, 2008).

22. Rebecca Bigler and Lynn S. Liben, "A Developmental Intergroup Theory of Social Stereotypes and Prejudices," *Advances in Child Development and Behavior* 34 (2006): 39–89; Thomas F. Pettigrew and Linda R. Tropp, "A Meta-Analytic Test of Intergroup Contact Theory," *Journal of Personality and Social Psychology* 90, no. 5 (2006): 751–83. See also Johanne Boisjoly et al., "Empathy or Antipathy? The Impact of Diversity," *American Economic Review* 96, no. 5 (2006): 1890–1905; Heidi McGlothlin and Melanie Killen, "How Social Experience Is Related to Children's Intergroup Attitudes," *European Journal of Social Psychology* 40, no. 4 (2010): 625; Adam Rutland et al., "Interracial Contact and Racial Constancy: A Multi-site Study of Racial Intergroup Bias in 3–5 Year Old Anglo-British Children," *Applied Developmental Psychology* 26 (2005): 699–713, https://kar.kent.ac.uk/26168/4/rutland%20et%20al%20JADP.pdf; Amy Stuart Wells and Robert L. Crain, "Perpetuation Theory and the Long-Term Effects of School Desegregation," *Review of Educational Research* 64, no. 4 (1994): 531–55.

23. Ming Ming Chiu and Lawrence Khoo, "Effects of Resources, Inequality, and Privilege Bias on Achievement: Country, School, and Student Level Analyses," *American Educational Research Journal* 42, no. 4 (2005): 575–603, http://aer.sagepub.com/content/42/4/575.abstract; Stephen W. Raudenbush, Randall P. Fotiu, and Yuk Fai Cheong, "Inequality of Access to Educational Resources: A National Report Card for Eighth-Grade Math," *Educational Evaluation and Policy Analysis* 20 (1998): 253–67, http://www.ssicentral.com/hlm/techdocs/EEPA98.pdf; Gary Orfield and Chungmei Lee, *Why Segregation Matters: Poverty and Educational Inequality,* Civil Rights Project, Harvard University, January 2005, http://civilrightsproject.ucla.edu/research/k-12-education/integration-and-diversity/why-segregation-matters-poverty-and-educational-inequality/orfield-why-segregation-matters-2005.pdf; Mark Schneider, "Do School Facilities Affect Academic Outcomes?" National Clearinghouse for Educational Facilities, November 2002, http://www.ncef.org/pubs/outcomes.pdf; Amy S. Wells et al., *Why Boundaries Matter: A Study of Five Separate and Unequal Long Island School Districts,* Center for Understanding Race and Education (CURE), Teachers College, Columbia University, July 2009, http://www.policyarchive.org/handle/10207/95995; Matthijs Kalmijn and Gerbert Kraaykamp, "Race, Cultural Capital, and Schooling: An Analysis of Trends in the United States," *Sociology of Education* 69 (1996): 22–34, https://www.jstor.org/stable/2112721?seq=1#page_scan_tab_contents; Jeffery Prager, Douglas Longshore, and Melvin Seeman, *School Desegregation Research: New Directions in Situational Analysis* (New York: Plenum Press, 1986), https://www.springer.com/us/book/9780306421518?.

24. Cynthia Duncan, *Worlds Apart: Why Poverty Persists in Rural America* (New Haven, CT: Yale University Press, 1999).

25. bell hooks, *Belonging: A Culture of Place* (London: Routledge, 2009).

26. bell hooks, *Teaching to Transgress: Education as the Practice of Freedom* (London: Routledge, 1994), 207.

27. Heidi Brocious et al., "The Strengths of Rural Social Workers: Perspectives on Managing Dual Relationships in Small Alaskan Communities," *Journal of Family Social Work* 16, no. 1 (2013): 4–19, doi:10.1080/10522158.2012.745180.

28. Mary L. Gray, *Out in the Country: Youth, Media, and Queer Visibility in Rural America* (New York: NYU Press, 2009).

29. Brocious et al., "The Strengths of Rural Social Workers." 6/29/20 7:18:00 PM

30. Kai A. Schafft, "Rural Education as Rural Development: Understanding the Rural School-Community Well-Being Linkage in a 21st-Century Policy Context," *Peabody Journal of Education* 91, no. 2 (2016): 137–54, doi:10.1080/01619 56X.2016.1151734.

31. Ben Court and Lachezar Manasiev, "Are Districts the Nation's Adolescent Mental Health Care Providers?" EAB, n.d., https://eab.com/research/ district-leadership/whitepaper/are-districts-the-nations-adolescent-mental-health-care-providers.

32. "School-Based Services Integration Model—Rural Services Integration Toolkit," Rural Health Information Hub, July 2012, https://www.ruralhealthinfo .org/toolkits/services-integration/2/school-based.

33. Kai T. Erikson, *Everything in Its Path: Destruction of Community in the Buffalo Creek Flood* (New York: Simon & Schuster, 1978).

34. Erikson.

35. Erikson.

36. Erikson, 234.

37. Hobarat Harmon and Kai Schafft, "Rural School Leadership for Collaborative Community Development," *Rural Educator* 30, no. 3 (2009): 4–9; Jerry W. Robinson Jr. and Gary Paul Green, *Introduction to Community Development: Theory, Practice, and Service-Learning* (Thousand Oaks, CA: Sage Publications, 2011).

38. Schafft, "Rural Education as Rural Development."

39. Schafft.

40. Robert M. Gibbs, Paul L. Swaim, and Ruy Teixeira, *Rural Education and Training in the New Economy: The Myth of the Rural Skills Gap* (Ames, IA: Iowa State University Press, 1998).

41. Sky Harmony Marietta, "Language, Literacy, and Place: Investigating Environment and Outcomes in Rural Appalachia" (EdD diss., Harvard University, 2012), http://search.proquest.com/pqdtglobal/docview/1268611311/abstract/97315AF DAE634CE3PQ/1.

42. Schafft, "Rural Education."

43. Deborah Erwin, "Ethnographic Description of Latino Immigration in Rural Arkansas: Intergroup Relations and Utilization of Healthcare Services," *Southern Rural Sociology* 19, no. 1 (2003): 46–72.

44. Schafft, "Rural Education."

45. David H. Monk, "Recruiting and Retaining High-Quality Teachers in Rural Areas," Future of Children 17, no. 1 (2007): 155–74, doi:10.1353/foc.2007.0009.

46. Monk.

47. Nat Malkus, Kathleen Mulvaney Hoyer, and Dinah Sparks, "Teaching Vacancies and Difficult-to-Staff Teaching Positions in Public Schools," Stats in Brief, NCES 2015-065, National Center for Education Statistics, 2015, http://eric.ed .gov/ERICWebPortal/detail?accno=ED561224.

48. Rhonda Barton, "Recruiting and Retaining Rural Educators: Challenges and Strategies," National Association of Secondary School Principals, Principal's Research Review 7, no. 6 (2012), https://educationnorthwest.org/sites/default/files/ resources/Principal%E2%80%99s%20Research%20Review%2C%20November %202012.pdf.

49. Monk, "Recruiting and Retaining"; Jared Coopersmith, "Characteristics of Public, Private, and Bureau of Indian Education Elementary and Secondary School Teachers in the United States: Results from the 2007–08 Schools and Staffing Survey: First Look," NCES 2009-324, National Center for Education Statistics, 2009, 1–65.

50. Charles T. Clotfelter, Helen Ladd, and Jacob L. Vigdor, "How and Why Do Teacher Credentials Matter for Student Achievement?," National Bureau of Economic Research, 2007, http://www.nber.org/papers/w12828.pdf.

51. Colleen Campbell, "Those Left Behind: Gaps in College Attainment by Race and Geography," Center for American Progress, June 27, 2019, https://www.american progress.org/issues/education-postsecondary/reports/2019/06/27/471242/ those-left-behind.

52. "Why Cultural Competence?," National Education Association, http://www .nea.org//home/39783.htm.

53. Julie Lynn Oliver, "The Story and Legacy of the Foxfire Cultural Journalism Program" (PhD diss., University of Georgia, 2011); Jamil Zainaldin, "Foxfire, Still Aglow—After Catastrophic Event, an Organization's Lessons Learned," SaportaReport (blog), November 2, 2015, https://saportareport.com/foxfire- still-aglow-after-catastrophic-event-an-organizations-lessons-learned.

54. Shirley Brice Heath, Ways with Words: Language, Life, and Work in Communities and Classrooms (Cambridge, England: Cambridge University Press, 1983).

55. Teresa L. McCarty, A Place to Be Navajo: Rough Rock and the Struggle for Self- Determination in Indigenous Schooling (New York: Routledge, 2002).

56. Duncan, Worlds Apart.

57. Ashley Welch, "Health Experts Say Parents Need to Drastically Cut Kids' Screen Time," CBS News, August 6, 2018, https://www.cbsnews.com/news/parents- need-to-drastically-cut-kids-screen-time-devices-american-heart-association.

58. Richard Louv, *Last Child in the Woods: Saving Our Children from Nature-Deficit Disorder*, updated and expanded ed. (Chapel Hill, NC: Algonquin Books, 2008); Angela J. Hanscom, *Balanced and Barefoot: How Unrestricted Outdoor Play Makes for Strong, Confident, and Capable Children* (Oakland, CA: New Harbinger Publications, 2016); Ainsley Arment, *The Call of the Wild and Free: Reclaiming Wonder in Your Child's Education* (San Francisco: HarperOne, 2019).

59. William H. Dietz, "The Obesity Epidemic in Young Children: Reduce Television Viewing and Promote Playing," *British Medical Journal* 322, no. 7282 (2001): 313–14; American Heart Association, "Children Living Near Green Spaces Are More Active," ScienceDaily, www.sciencedaily.com/releases/2009/03/090312114757.htm.

60. Dietz, "The Obesity Epidemic"; American Heart Association, "Children Living Near Green Spaces"; Aspen Institute Sports & Society Program, *Sport for All, Play for Life: A Playbook to Get Every Kid in the Game*, Aspen Institute, 2015, https://www.aspeninstitute.org/publications/sport-all-play-life-playbook-get-every-kid-game/.

61. Linda Burton et al., "Working with African American Clients: Considering the 'Homeplace' in Marriage and Family Therapy Practices," *Journal of Marital and Family Therapy* 30 (November 1, 2004): 397–410, doi:10.1111/j.1752-0606.2004.tb01251.x; bell hooks, *Yearning: Race, Gender, and Cultural Politics* (New York: Routledge, 2014) .

62. Craig B. Howley and Aimee Howley, "Poverty and School Achievement in Rural Communities: A Social-Class Interpretation," in *Rural Education for the Twenty-first Century*, ed. Kai A. Schafft and Alecia Youngblood Jackson (University Park, PA: Penn State University Press, 2010).

63. hooks, *Belonging*.

64. Sunshine Brosi and Sky Marietta, "Experiential Trips to Help Appalachian Students Persist Toward Primary Degrees in the Sciences," *Journal of Appalachian Studies* 25, no. 1 (2019): 105–15, www.jstor.org/stable/10.5406/jappastud.25.1.0105.

Chapter 3

1. Dan Chekki, ed., *New Communities in a Changing World*, Research in Community Sociology, vol. 6 (Bingley, UK: Emerald Group Publishing, 1996).

2. Colin Woodard, *American Nations: A History of the Eleven Rival Regional Cultures of North America* (New York: Viking, 2011); David Hackett Fischer, *Albion's Seed: Four British Folkways in America* (New York: Oxford University Press, 1989).

3. Annie Baxter, "How an Immigration Raid Threw a Small Iowa Town into Economic Crisis," *Marketplace* (blog), August 3, 2017, https://www.marketplace.org/2017/08/03/postvilles-long-recovery-after-raid.

4. Joy Minikwu, "Lessons from Postville: How an Immigration Raid Changed a Small Town and Its Schools," Colorín Colorado, February 22, 2017, https://www.colorincolorado.org/article/lessons-postville-how-immigration-raid-changed-small-town-and-its-schools.

5. Mara Casey Tieken, Why Rural Schools Matter (Chapel Hill, NC: University of North Carolina Press, 2014).

6. Alex Granados, "Education, Unsettled: The Struggle to Keep Migrant Students in School," Education Week, November 28, 2018, https://www.edweek.org/ew/projects/education-unsettled-migrant-students.html?cmp=SOC-SHR-FB.

7. Tennessee Watson, "The Children in the Fields," APM Reports, August 14, 2019, https://www.apmreports.org/story/2019/08/14/the-children-in-the-fields.

8. "US Department of Education Fiscal Year 2020 Budget Summary," US Department of Education, https://www2.ed.gov/about/overview/budget/budget20/summary/20summary.pdf.

9. "US Department of Education Fiscal Year 2020."

10. Nadra Nittle, "For Children of Migrant Farmworkers, High School Graduation Takes a Village," Salon, July 14, 2019, https://www.salon.com/2019/07/14/for-children-of-migrant-farmworkers-high-school-graduation-takes-a-village_partner.

11. NPR, "New Boom Reshapes Oil World, Rocks North Dakota," All Things Considered, NPR.org, September 25, 2011, https://www.npr.org/2011/09/25/140784004/new-boom-reshapes-oil-world-rocks-north-dakota.

12. Nathan Ratledge and Laura Zachary, "The Impact of Shale Oil Development on Public Education in North Dakota," Resources, June 16, 2016, https://www.resourcesmag.org/common-resources/the-impact-of-shale-oil-development-on-public-education-in-north-dakota.

13. "Eastern N.D. Schools Impacted by Oil Boom, See Growth," Grand Forks Herald, November 22, 2013, https://www.grandforksherald.com/news/2203259-eastern-nd-schools-impacted-oil-boom-see-growth.

14. Ratledge and Zachary, "The Impact of Shale Oil Development."

15. Peter F. Korsching and John C. Allen, "Locality Based Entrepreneurship: A Strategy for Community Economic Vitality," Community Development Journal 39, no. 4 (2004): 385–400, doi:10.1093/cdj/bsh034.

16. Milena Nikolova and Boris N. Nikolaev, "Family Matters: The Effects of Parental Unemployment in Early Childhood and Adolescence on Subjective Well-Being Later in Life," Journal of Economic Behavior and Organization, May 26, 2018, doi:10.1016/j.jebo.2018.05.005.

17. Loring Jones, "The Effect of Unemployment on Children and Adolescents," Children and Youth Services Review 10, no. 3 (1988): 199–215.

18. Kai A. Schafft, "Rural Education as Rural Development: Understanding the Rural School-Community Well-Being Linkage in a 21st-Century Policy

Context," *Peabody Journal of Education* 91, no. 2 (2016): 137–54, doi:10.1080/01619
56X.2016.1151734.

19. Michael Corbett, *Learning to Leave: The Irony of Schooling in a Coastal Community* (Halifax, NS: Fernwood Publishing, 2007).

20. Corbett, *Learning to Leave*Michael Corbett, "Rural Education and Out-Migration: The Case of a Coastal Community," *Canadian Journal of Education* 28, no. 1/2 (2005): 52–73, doi:10.2307/1602153.

21. Patrick J. Carr and Maria J. Kefalas, *Hollowing Out the Middle: The Rural Brain Drain and What It Means for America* (Boston, MA: Beacon Press, 2010).6/29/20 7:18:00 PM

22. "Where Americans Find Meaning in Life," Pew Research Center, November 20, 2018, https://www.pewforum.org/2018/11/20/where-americans-find-meaning-in-life.

23. Schafft, "Rural Education as Rural Development."

24. See Joel M. Hektner, "When Moving Up Implies Moving Out: Rural Adolescent Conflict in the Transition to Adulthood," *Journal of Research in Rural Education* 11, no. 1 (1995): 3–14.

25. "Eastern N.D. Schools Impacted by Oil Boom, See Growth"; NPR, "New Boom Reshapes Oil World."

26. "A Rural Brain Gain Migration," University of Minnesota Extension, https://extension.umn.edu/economic-development/rural-brain-gain-migration.

27. Niall McCarthy, "India Lifted 271 Million People Out of Poverty in a Decade," *Forbes*, July 12, 2019, https://www.forbes.com/sites/niallmccarthy/2019/07/12/report-india-lifted-271-million-people-out-of-poverty-in-a-decade-infographic.

28. Katie Canales, "An 'Urban Flight' from the San Francisco Bay Area Could Be Accelerated as More People Work Remotely in the Future and Flock to Less Expensive US Cities," Business Insider, May 14, 2020, https://www.businessinsider.com/pandemic-urban-flight-people-leaving-silicon-valley-coronavirus-2020-5.

29. Kim Hart, "Coronavirus May Prompt Migration Out of American Cities," Axios, April 30, 2020, https://www.axios.com/coronavirus-migration-american-cities-survey-aba181ba-a4ce-45b2-931c-6c479889ad37.html.

30. Roman Ruiz and Laura W Perna, "The Geography of College Attainment: Dismantling Rural 'Disadvantage,'" Pell Institute and PennAHEAD, 2017, http://pellinstitute.org/indicators/downloads/dialogues-2017_essays_Ruiz_Perna.pdf.

31. Kelvin Pollard and Linda A. Jacobsen, *The Appalachian Region: A Data Overview from the 2006–2010 American Community Survey* (Washington, DC: Appalachian Regional Commission, 2012), https://www.arc.gov/assets/research_reports/PRB-DataOverview-2012.pdf.

32. Thomas A. Lyson, "Big Business and Community Welfare," *American Journal of Economics and Sociology* 65, no. 5 (November 2006): 1001–23,

doi:10.1111/j.1536-7150.2006.00489.x; Melville Ulmer and C. Wright Mills, *Small Business and Civic Welfare: Report of the Smaller War Plants Corporation to the Special Committee to Study Problems of American Small Business*, US Senate, 79th Congress, 2nd Session (Washington, DC: US Government Printing Office, 1946); Charles M. Tolbert, Thomas A. Lyson, and Michael D. Irwin, "Local Capitalism, Civic Engagement, and Socioeconomic Well-Being," *Social Forces* 77, no. 2 (1998): 401–27.

33. Manley A. Begay Jr., Stephen Cornell, Miriam Jorgensen, and Joseph P. Kalt, "Development, Governance, Culture: What Are They and What Do They Have to Do with Rebuilding Native Nations?," in *Rebuilding Native Nations*, ed. Miriam Jorgensen (Tucson, AZ: University of Arizona Press, 2007).

34. Michael P. Conzen, ed., *The Making of the American Landscape*, 2nd ed. (New York: Routledge, 2010).

35. NPR, "The Navajo Nation's Own 'Trail Of Tears,'" *All Things Considered*, NPR.org, June 14, 2005, https://www.npr.org/2005/06/15/4703136/the-navajo-nation-s-own-trail-of-tears.

36. Julie Davis, "American Indian Boarding School Experiences: Recent Studies for Native Perspectives," *Magazine of History* 15, no. 2 (2001): 20–22, doi:10.1093/maghis/15.2.20.

Chapter 4

1. James J. Heckman, "Invest in Early Childhood Development: Reduce Deficits, Strengthen the Economy," Heckman Equation, December 7, 2012, https://heckmanequation.org/www/assets/2013/07/F_HeckmanDeficitPieceCUSTOM-Generic_052714-3-1.pdf.

2. Hirokazu Yoshikawa et al., "Investing in Our Future: The Evidence Base on Preschool Education," Society for Research in Child Development, October 2013, http://eric.ed.gov/ERICWebPortal/detail?accno=ED579818.

3. Catherine E. Snow et al., Is Literacy Enough? Pathways to Academic Success for Adolescents (Baltimore, MD: Paul H. Brookes Publishing, 2007).

4. Brittany L. Rhoades et al., "Demographic and Familial Predictors of Early Executive Function Development: Contribution of a Person-Centered Perspective," Journal of Experimental Child Psychology 108, no. 3 (2011): 638–62, doi:10.1016/j.jecp.2010.08.004.

5. Snow et al., Is Literacy Enough?

6. Lynne Vernon-Feagans and Martha Cox, "The Family Life Project: An Epidemiological and Developmental Study of Young Children Living in Poor Rural Communities," Monographs of the Society for Research in Child Development 78, no. 5 (2013): 1–126, doi:10.1111/mono.12047.

7. Jodi Berger Cardoso and Sanna J. Thompson, "Common Themes of Resilience Among Latino Immigrant Families: A Systematic Review of the Literature,"

Families in Society 91, no. 3 (2010): 257–65.

8. Deborah Erwin, "An Ethnographic Description of Latino Immigration in Rural Arkansas: Intergroup Relations and Utilization of Healthcare Services," *Southern Rural Sociology* 19, no. 1 (2003): 46–72.6/29/20 7:18:00 PM

9. Nonie K. Lesaux et al., "Turning the Page: Refocusing Massachusetts for Reading Success," Strategies for Children, 2010, http://www.strategiesforchildren.org/docs_research/10_TurningThePageReport.pdf.

10. Heckman, "Invest in Early Childhood Development."

11. NPR did a great feature on Martin County fifty years after Johnson's visit. Access the article and radio story at https://www.npr.org/2014/01/08/260151923/kentucky-county-that-gave-war-on-poverty-a-face-still-struggles.

12. Jay Belsky et al., "Are There Long-Term Effects of Early Child Care?," *Child Development* 78, no. 2 (2007): 681–701; William T. Gormley Jr. et al., "The Effects of Universal Pre-K on Cognitive Development," *Developmental Psychology* 41, no. 6 (2005): 872–84.

13. Heckman, "Invest in Early Childhood Development."

14. Eric Westervelt, "How Investing In Preschool Beats The Stock Market, Hands Down," NPR.org, December 12, 2016, https://www.npr.org/sections/ed/2016/12/12/504867570/how-investing-in-preschool-beats-the-stock-market-hands-down.

15. Rasheed Malik and Katie Hamm, "Mapping America's Child Care Deserts," Center for American Progress, August 30, 2017, http://search.proquest.com/docview/1946287280/?pq-origsite=primo.

16. Vernon-Feagans and Cox, "The Family Life Project."

17. Erik Ruzek et al., "The Quality of Toddler Child Care and Cognitive Skills at 24 Months: Propensity Score Analysis Results from the ECLS-B," *Early Childhood Research Quarterly* 28, no. 1 (2014), doi:10.1016/j.ecresq.2013.09.002; Yoshikawa et al., "Investing in Our Future"; Allison Friedman-Krauss, W. Steven Barnett, and Milagros Nores, "How Much Can High-Quality Universal Pre-K Reduce Achievement Gaps?," Center for American Progress, April 5, 2016, https://www.americanprogress.org/issues/education/report/2016/04/05/132750/how-much-can-high-quality-universal-pre-k-reduce-achievement-gaps.

18. In a series of papers for the Minneapolis Fed, Rolnick and Grunewald proposed that investment in early childhood development achieved high economic returns and that high-quality services could be achieved using a market-based scholarship to drive demand. For more information see Stacey Childress and Geoff Marietta, "Investing in Early Learning as Economic Development at the Minneapolis Federal Reserve Bank" (HBS Case No. 309-090, Harvard Business School, Boston, 2009).

19. Stacey Childress and Geoff Marietta, "Invest Early: Early Childhood Development in a Rural Community" (HBS Case No. 309-089, Harvard Business School, Boston, 2009).

20. The NIEER Quality Benchmarks can be found at http://nieer.org/wp-content/uploads/2019/02/CPQR4_Quality-Standards-e-2019_01_30.pdf.

21. Alice McIntyre, *Participatory Action Research (Qualitative Research Methods)* (Thousand Oaks, CA: Sage Publications, 2008).

Chapter 5

1. Sylvia Ashton-Warner, *Teacher* (New York: Simon & Schuster, 1963).

2. Eliot Wigginton, *The Foxfire Book* (New York: Anchor Books, 1972).

3. Teresa L. McCarty, *A Place to Be Navajo* (New York: Routledge, 2002).

4. Lynne Vernon-Feagans and Martha Cox, "The Family Life Project: An Epidemiological and Developmental Study of Young Children Living in Poor Rural Communities," *Monographs of the Society for Research in Child Development* 78, no. 5 (2013): 1–126, doi:10.1111/mono.12047.

5. Michael J. Kieffer and Nonie K. Lesaux, "Morphing Into Adolescents: Active Word Learning for English-Language Learners and Their Classmates in Middle School," *Journal of Adolescent & Adult Literacy* 54, no. 1 (2010): 47–56, doi:10.1598/JAAL.54.1.5.

6. Andrew Biemiller and Naomi Slonim, "Estimating Root Word Vocabulary Growth in Normative and Advantaged Populations: Evidence for a Common Sequence of Vocabulary Acquisition," *Journal of Educational Psychology* 93, no. 3 (September 2001): 498–520, doi:10.1037/0022-0663.93.3.498.

7. Catherine E. Snow et al., *Is Literacy Enough? Pathways to Academic Success for Adolescents* (Baltimore, MD: Paul H. Brookes Publishing, 2007).

8. Todd R. Risley and Betty Hart, *Meaningful Differences in the Everyday Experience of Young American Children* (Baltimore, MD: Paul H. Brookes Publishing, 1995).

9. Douglas E. Sperry, Linda L. Sperry, and Peggy J. Miller, "Reexamining the Verbal Environments of Children from Different Socioeconomic Backgrounds," *Child Development* 90, no. 4 (2019): 1303–18, doi:10.1111/cdev.13072.

10. Tim Shanahan has a great discussion on his blog: "Is There Really a 30 Million-Word Gap?," *Shanahan on Literacy* (blog), September 8, 2018, https://shanahanonliteracy.com/blog/is-there-really-a-30-million-word-gap.

11. Snow et al., *Is Literacy Enough?*

12. Nonie Lesaux and Sky Marietta, *Making Assessment Matter: Using Test Results to Differentiate Instruction* (New York: Guilford Press, 2012).

13. Lisa Delpit and Joanne Kilgour Dowdy, *The Skin That We Speak: Thoughts on Language and Culture in the Classroom* (New York: New Press, 2002); Patrick J. Finn, *Literacy with an Attitude: Educating Working-Class Children in Their Own Self-Interest*, 2nd ed. (Albany: SUNY Press, 2009); James Paul Gee, "Literacy, Discourse, and Linguistics: Introduction," *Journal of Education* 171, no. 1 (1989): 5–17, doi:10.1177/002205748917100101; Shirley Brice Heath, *Ways with Words: Language, Life, and Work in Communities and Classrooms* (Cambridge,

England: Cambridge University Press, 1983); Peggy J. Miller, Grace E. Cho, and Jeana R. Bracey, "Working-Class Children's Experience Through the Prism of Personal Storytelling," *Human Development* 48, no. 3 (2005): 115–35, doi:10.1159/000085515.

14. Lynne Vernon-Feagans and Martha Cox, "The Family Life Project: An Epidemiological and Developmental Study of Young Children Living in Poor Rural Communities," *Monographs of the Society for Research in Child Development* 78, no. 5 (2013): 1–126, doi:10.1111/mono.12047.

15. Heath, *Ways with Words*.

16. Lowry Hemphill, "Topic Development, Syntax, and Social Class," *Discourse Processes* 12, no. 3 (1989): 267–86, doi:10.1080/01638538909544731; Deborah Hicks, *Reading Lives: Working-Class Children and Literacy Learning*, Language and Literacy Series (New York: Teachers College Press, 2001); Sarah Michaels, "The Dismantling of Narrative," in *Developing Narrative Structure*, ed. Allyssa McCabe and Carole Peterson (Hillsdale, NJ: Lawrence Erlbaum, 1991), 303–51.

17. Elsa Auerbach, "Toward a Social-Contextual Approach to Family Literacy," *Harvard Educational Review* 59, no. 2 (1989): 165, doi:10.17763/haer.59.2 .h237313641283156; Sarah Michaels, "'Sharing Time': Children's Narrative Styles and Differential Access to Literacy," *Language in Society* 10, no. 3 (1981): 423–42, doi:10.1017/S0047404500008861; Lisa D. Delpit, "Acquisition of Literate Discourse: Bowing Before the Master?," *Theory into Practice* 31, no. 4 (1992): 296–302, doi:10.1080/00405849209543556; Gee, "Literacy, Discourse, and Linguistics."

18. Peter F. de Jong and Paul P. M. Leseman, "Lasting Effects of Home Literacy on Reading Achievement in School," *Journal of School Psychology* 39, no. 5 (2001): 389–414, doi:10.1016/S0022-4405(01)00080-2; David K. Dickinson and Allyssa McCabe, "Bringing It All Together: The Multiple Origins, Skills, and Environmental Supports of Early Literacy," *Learning Disabilities Research & Practice* 16, no. 4 (2001): 186–202, doi:10.1111/0938-8982.00019; Betty Hart, *Meaningful Differences in the Everyday Experience of Young American Children* (Baltimore, MD: Paul H. Brookes Publishing, 1995); Stacey Storch and Grover Whitehurst, "The Role of Family and Home in the Literacy Development of Children from Low-Income Backgrounds," *New Directions for Child and Adolescent Development* 92, summer (2001): 53–71.

19. Mary J. Schleppegrell, *The Language of Schooling: A Functional Linguistics Perspective* (Mahwah, NJ: Lawrence Erlbaum, 2004).

20. Luis Moll et al., "Funds of Knowledge for Teaching: Using a Qualitative Approach to Connect Homes and Classrooms," *Theory into Practice* 31, no. 2 (1992): 132–41.

21. Helen Raikes et al., "Mother–Child Bookreading in Low-Income Families: Correlates and Outcomes During the First Three Years of Life," *Child*

Development 77, no. 4 (2006): 924–53, doi:10.1111/j.1467-8624.2006.00911.x; William H. Teale and Elizabeth Sulzby, eds., *Emergent Literacy: Writing and Reading* (Westport, CT: Ablex Publishing, 1986).

22. Zo Weizman and C. E. Snow, "Lexical Input as Related to Children's Vocabulary Acquisition: Effects of Sophisticated Exposure and Support for Meaning," *Developmental Psychology* 37, no. 2 (2001): 265–79, doi:10.1037//0012-1649.37.2.265.

23. National Research Council, *Preventing Reading Difficulties in Young Children* (Washington, DC: National Academies Press, 1998).

24. Auerbach, "Toward a Social-Contextual Approach to Family Literacy."

25. S. B. Neuman and D. Celano, "Access to Print in Low-Income and Middle-Income Communities: An Ecological Study of Four Neighborhoods," *Reading Research Quarterly* 36, no. 1 (2001): 8–26.

26. Jen Fifield, "Yes, Bookmobiles Are Still a Thing. (We Checked.)," *Stateline*, an initiative of the Pew Charitable Trusts, March 28, 2018, https://www.pewtrusts.org/en/research-and-analysis/blogs/stateline/2018/03/28/yes-bookmobiles-are-still-a-thing-we-checked.

27. Mara Casey Tieken, *Why Rural Schools Matter* (Chapel Hill, NC: University of North Carolina Press, 2014).

28. Nagy and Townsend, "Words as Tools."

29. National Research Council, *Preventing Reading Difficulties in Young Children*.

30. Michaels, "'Sharing Time.'"

31. Elizabeth B. Moje, Deborah R. Dillon, and David O'Brien, "Reexamining Roles of Learner, Text, and Context in Secondary Literacy," *Journal of Educational Research* 93, no. 3 (2000): 165–80, doi:10.1080/00220670009598705.

32. Lisa D. Delpit, "The Silenced Dialogue: Power and Pedagogy in Educating Other People's Children," *Harvard Educational Review* 58, no. 3 (1988): 280–98, doi:10.17763/haer.58.3.c43481778r528qw4.

33. Auerbach, "Toward a Social-Contextual Approach to Family Literacy"; Basil Bernstein, "Education Cannot Compensate for Society," *New Society* 387 (1970): 344–47; Shirley Brice Heath, "Re-Creating Literature in the ESL Classroom," *TESOL Quarterly* 30, no. 4 (1996): 776–79, doi:10.2307/3587935; Phyllis A. Miller, "Reading Demands in a High-Technology Industry," *Journal of Reading* 26, no. 2 (1982): 109–15; Michaels, "'Sharing Time.'"

34. Scarcella, "Academic English"; Mary J. Schleppegrell, "Linguistic Features of the Language of Schooling," *Linguistics and Education* 12, no. 4 (2001): 431–59, doi:10.1016/S0898-5898(01)00073-0.

Chapter 6

1. National Science Foundation, "What Percentage of Freshmen Intend to Major in an S&E Field When They Start College?," National Science Foundation, 2014, https://www.nsf.gov/nsb/sei/edTool/data/college-09.html.

2. National Science Foundation.
3. Chris McGreal, "Obama's State of the Union Address: US Must Seize 'Sputnik Moment,'" *The Guardian*, January 26, 2011, sec. US news, https://www.theguardian.com/world/2011/jan/26/state-of-the-union-address-obama-sputnik-moment.
4. Judith Hallinen, "STEM Education Curriculum," in *Encyclopædia Britannica*, June 28, 2019, https://www.britannica.com/topic/STEM-education.
5. Linda Jacobson, "Ohio Initiative Adds to STEM Momentum," *Education Week*, January 31, 2008, https://www.edweek.org/ew/articles/2008/02/06/22stem.h27.html?qs=STEM.
6. "Ohio STEM Learning Network History," Ohio STEM Learning Network, March 12, 2013, https://osln.org/about/history.
7. "About the STEMx™ Network," STEMx, January 8, 2013, https://stemx.us/about.
8. Anne Jolly, "STEM vs. STEAM: Do the Arts Belong?," *Education Week—Teacher*, November 18, 2014, https://www.edweek.org/tm/articles/2014/11/18/ctq-jolly-stem-vs-steam.html; Anna Feldman, "Why We Need to Put the Arts into STEM Education," *Slate*, June 16, 2015, https://slate.com/technology/2015/06/steam-vs-stem-why-we-need-to-put-the-arts-into-stem-education.html.
9. Kate Kastelein et al., "The 2018 Rural Informal STEM Conference: Final Report," Maine Mathematics and Science Alliance, 2018, https://www.mmsa.org/projects/RuralConference2018.
10. "Broadband Speed Guide," Federal Communications Commission, August 1, 2011, https://www.fcc.gov/consumers/guides/broadband-speed-guide.
11. Joshua Bleiberg, "Are School Internet Connections Fast Enough to Support Personalized Learning?," *Brookings* (blog), June 15, 2016, https://www.brookings.edu/blog/brown-center-chalkboard/2016/06/15/are-school-internet-connections-fast-enough-to-support-personalized-learning.
12. Roger Riddell, "Is E-Rate Doing Enough to Effectively Expand Broadband in Rural Schools?," *Education Dive*, March 23, 2018, https://www.educationdive.com/news/is-e-rate-doing-enough-to-effectively-expand-broadband-in-rural-schools/519788.
13. Nichole Dobo, "Most Students Go to a School That Meets Federal Standards for Internet Speed," *Hechinger Report* (blog), January 18, 2017, https://hechingerreport.org/students-go-school-meets-federal-standards-internet-speed/.
14. John B. Horrigan, "The Numbers Behind the Broadband 'Homework Gap,'" Pew Research Center, Fact Tank, April 20, 2015, https://www.pewresearch.org/fact-tank/2015/04/20/the-numbers-behind-the-broadband-homework-gap.
15. Horrigan.
16. Angelina Kewalramani et al., "Student Access to Digital Learning Resources Outside of the Classroom," NCES 2017-098, National Center for Education Statistics, 2018, http://eric.ed.gov/ERICWebPortal/detail?accno=ED581891.
17. Monica Anderson and Andrew Perrin, "Nearly One-in-Five Teens Can't

Always Finish Their Homework Because of the Digital Divide," Pew Research Center, Fact Tank, October 26, 2018, https://www.pewresearch.org/fact-tank/ 2018/10/26/nearly-one-in-five-teens-cant-always-finish-their-homework-because-of-the-digital-divide; Jessica Rosenworcel, "Bridging the Homework Gap," HuffPost, June 15, 2015, https://www.huffpost.com/entry/bridging-the-homework-gap_b_7590042.

18. "Taking the Pulse of the High School Student Experience in America," Family Online Safety Institute, April 29, 2015, https://www.fosi.org/documents/142/ Taking_the_Pulse_Phase_1_Research_Findings_FINAL.pdf.

19. Jessica Fregni, "This Community Set Out to Bridge the Digital Divide," Teach for America, January 21, 2020, https://www.teachforamerica.org/stories/this-community-set-out-to-bridge-the-digital-divide.

20. Fregni.

21. Kewalramani et al., "Student Access to Digital Learning Resources."

22. Allen Pratt, "The Digital Divide Leaves Rural Students Behind, Innovation Can Change That," The Hill, September 3, 2019, https://thehill.com/blogs/congress-blog/technology/459809-the-digital-divide-leaves-rural-students-behind-innovation-can.

23. Brian Sponsler et al., "Advanced Placement Access and Success: How Do Rural Schools Stack Up?," Education Commission of the States, http://search.proquest .com/docview/1958457980/?pq-origsite=primo.

24. Zahra Hazari et al., "Connecting High School Physics Experiences, Outcome Expectations, Physics Identity, and Physics Career Choice: A Gender Study," Journal of Research in Science Teaching 47, no. 8 (2010): 978–1003, doi:10.1002/ tea.20363; Terry L. Sharik et al., "Undergraduate Enrollment in Natural Resource Programs in the United States: Trends, Drivers, and Implications for the Future of Natural Resource Professions," Journal of Forestry 113, no. 6 (2015): 538–51, doi:10.5849/jof.14-146.

25. Google Inc. and Gallup Inc., "Computer Science Learning: Closing the Gap: Rural and Small Town School Districts," August 2017, http://services.google .com/fh/files/misc/computer-science-learning-closing-the-gap-rural-small-town-brief.pdf.

26. Google Inc. and Gallup Inc.

27. "About TEALS—What Is TEALS?," Microsoft, https://www.microsoft.com/ en-us/teals/about.

28. Kate Stringer, "In These Rural Schools, the Computer Science Teachers Are Volunteers Who Work for Microsoft, Amazon and Google. That's Opening Doors for Their Students," May 6, 2019, the74million.org, https://www.the74 million.org/article/in-these-rural-schools-the-computer-science-teachers-are-volunteers-who-work-for-microsoft-amazon-and-google-thats-opening-doors-for-their-students.

29. Stringer.

30. Michael Noer, "One Man, One Computer, 10 Million Students: How Khan Academy Is Reinventing Education," Forbes, November 19, 2012, https://www .forbes.com/sites/michaelnoer/2012/11/02/one-man-one-computer-10-million-students-how-khan-academy-is-reinventing-education.

31. "Khan Academy Founder Heralds Nation's First Statewide Pilot in Idaho," J. A. and Kathryn Albertson Family Foundation, February 28, 2013, https://www.jkaf.org/news/khan-academy-founder-heralds-nations-first-statewide-pilot-in-idaho.

32. "College Board's Expanding Commitment to Rural Students," College Board, October 1, 2019, https://www.collegeboard.org/membership/all-access/counseling-admissions-financial-aid-academic/college-board-s-expanding.

33. Bernhard Schroeder, "Disrupting Education. The Rise of K-12 Online and the Entrepreneurial Opportunities," Forbes, August 14, 2019, https://www.forbes .com/sites/bernhardschroeder/2019/08/14/disrupting-education-the-rise-of-k-12-online-and-the-entrepreneurial-opportunities.

34. "Introducing the Rural Spark Project: A Chance for Rural Students to Have Bright Futures in STEM," September 5, 2017, https://www.3blmedia.com/News/Introducing-Rural-Spark-Project-Chance-Rural-Students-Have-Bright-Futures-STEM.

35. "Chevron Appalachia Gives $70,000 to Local Schools for Project Lead The Way," TimesReporter.com, January 23, 2019, https://www.timesreporter.com/news/20190123/chevron-appalachia-gives-70000-to-local-schools-for-project-lead-way.

36. "Charting a Course for Success: America's Strategy for STEM Education," STEM Ecosystems, https://stemecosystems.org.

37. New Tech Network, https://newtechnetwork.org.

38. Richard Riley, "Is This the Way to Transform Struggling Rural Schools?," Hechinger Report (blog), May 24, 2018, https://hechingerreport.org/opinion-is-this-the-way-to-transform-struggling-rural-schools/.

39. "The Infinity Project," https://www.smu.edu/Lyle/Institutes/CaruthInstitute/K-12Programs/InfinityProject.

40. "K-12 Outreach," Vanderbilt Institute of Nanoscale Science and Engineering, https://www.vanderbilt.edu/vinse/outreach.php.

41. "Lab-in-a-Box and Rural Communities STEM Initiative," Roane State Community College, https://www.roanestate.edu/?10681-Lab-in-a-Box-and-Rural-Communities-STEM-Initiative.

42. "Dartmouth Rural STEM Educator Partnership—An Educational Outreach Project Funded by SEPA-NIGMS," Dartmouth College, https://sites.dartmouth .edu/sepa.

43. https://battelleforkids.org/docs/default-source/publications/generatingopportunityprosperityview.pdf.

44. "Generating Opportunity and Prosperity."
45. Golden Triangle Cooperative, https://www.gtccmt.org.
46. "Ohio Appalachian Collaborative," Battelle for Kids, http://portal.battelleforkids
    .org/OAC/our-purpose/personalized-learning-pathways/course-offerings#stem.
47. "Kentucky Valley Educational Cooperative," KVEC, https://www.kentuckyvalley
    .org/about.
48. Ron Daley, "Kentucky Valley Educational Cooperative Prepares to Celebrate
    Its 50th Birthday," The Holler, August 20, 2018, https://www.theholler.org/
    kentuckys-oldest-k-12-cooperative-the-kentucky-valley-educational-cooper-
    ative-prepares-to-celebrate-its-50th-birthday.
49. Daley.
50. "2018/2019 Speakers," FIREsummit, https://summit.theholler.org/2018-2019-
    speakers.
51. "North Carolina School of Science and Mathematics—About NCSSM," https://
    www.ncssm.edu/about.
52. "North Carolina School of Science and Mathematics—Competitions & Events,"
    https://www.ncssm.edu/residential-program/academics/competitions-events.
53. "North Carolina School of Science and Mathematics—STEM Scholars Program,"
    https://www.ncssm.edu/for-nc-schools/nc-public-schools/stem-scholars-
    program.
54. "North Carolina School of Science and Mathematics—K-9 STEM Enrich-
    ments," https://www.ncssm.edu/stemenrichments.
55. Gatton Academy for Mathematics and Science, https://www.wku.edu/academy/
    documents/2019_recruitment_profile.pdf.
56. Craft Academy for Excellence in Science and Math, https://www.morehead
    state.edu/Academics/Craft-Academy/About-Craft-Academy.
57. Laurel County Schools Center for Innovation, https://www.laurel.kyschools
    .us/19/Content2/1618.
58. Laurel County Schools Center for Innovation.
59. "Our Membership," National FFA Organization, https://www.ffa.org/our-
    membership.
60. "National FFA Career And Leadership Development Events Handbook,"
    National FFA Organization, https://ffa.app.box.com/s/vpx52yly9mpiai35srdzl
    7oq68kldnbt.
61. "Microsoft and National FFA Bring Technology to Rural America; Students
    Attending National FFA Convention Experience It First-Hand," National FFA
    Organization, https://www.ffa.org/press-releases/microsoft-and-national-ffa-
    bring-technology-to-rural-america-students-attending-national-ffa-convention-
    experience-it-first-hand.
62. "Science, Technology, Engineering, & Math Curriculum," 4-H, https://shop4-h
    .org/collections/science-technology-engineering-math-curriculum.

Chapter 7

1. Andrew Crain, "Serving Rural Students," National Association of Colleges and Employers, May 1, 2018, https://www.naceweb.org/career-development/special-populations/serving-rural-students.
2. National Center for Education Statistics, "The Status of Rural Education," May 2013, https://nces.ed.gov/programs/coe/indicator_tla.asp.
3. USDA, Economic Research Service, "Rural Education," https://www.ers.usda.gov/topics/rural-economy-population/employment-education/rural-education.
4. Emmie Martin, "Home Prices Have Risen 114% Since 1960—Here's How Much More Expensive Life Is Today," CNBC, April 17, 2018, https://www.cnbc.com/2018/04/17/how-much-more-expensive-life-is-today-than-it-was-in-1960.html.
5. Matt Krupnick, "Economics, Culture and Distance Conspire to Keep Rural Nonwhites from Higher Educations," Hechinger Report, January 18, 2018, https://hechingerreport.org/eclipsed-urban-counterparts-rural-nonwhites-go-college-equally-low-rates.
6. National Center for Education Statistics, "Public High School Graduation Rates," May 2019, https://nces.ed.gov/programs/coe/indicator_coi.asp.
7. Daniel Showalter et al., "Why Rural Matters 2015–2016: Understanding the Changing Landscape. A Report of the Rural School and Community Trust," Rural School and Community Trust, 2017, http://eric.ed.gov/ERICWebPortal/detail?accno=ED590169; National Center for Education Statistics, "Public High School."
8. USDA, Economic Research Service, "Rural Education."
9. USDA, Economic Research Service.
10. USDA, Economic Research Service.
11. Krupnick, "Economics, Culture and Distance."
12. US Bureau of Labor Statistics, "Unemployment Rates and Earnings by Educational Attainment, 2018," https://www.bls.gov/emp/graphics/2019/unemployment-rates-and-earnings.htm.
13. US Bureau of Labor Statistics.
14. World Economic Forum, "The Future of Jobs Report 2018," 2018, http://www3.weforum.org/docs/WEF_Future_of_Jobs_2018.pdf.
15. Crain, "Serving Rural Students."
16. National Center for Education Statistics, "The Status of Rural Education."
17. National Center for Education Statistics, "Rural Education in America," https://nces.ed.gov/surveys/ruraled/tables/b.3.b.-1.asp.
18. Carrie Dann, "Americans Split on Value of 4-Year College Degree," NBC News, September 7, 2017, https://www.nbcnews.com/politics/first-read/americans-split-whether-4-year-college-degree-worth-cost-n799336.

19. Rich Morin, "Behind Trump's Win in Rural White America," Pew Research Center, Fact Tank, November 17, 2016, https://www.pewresearch.org/fact-tank/2016/11/17/behind-trumps-win-in-rural-white-america-women-joined-men-in-backing-him.

20. Emmie Martin, "Here's How Much More Expensive It Is for You to Go to College Than It Was for Your Parents," CNBC, November 29, 2017, https://www.cnbc.com/2017/11/29/how-much-college-tuition-has-increased-from-1988-to-2018.html.

21. Drew Desilver, "For Most Americans, Real Wages Have Barely Budged for Decades," Pew Research Center, Fact Tank, August 7, 2018, https://www.pewresearch.org/fact-tank/2018/08/07/for-most-us-workers-real-wages-have-barely-budged-for-decades.

22. Saba Rasheed Ali and Jodi L. Saunders, "The Career Aspirations of Rural Appalachian High School Students," *Journal of Career Assessment* 17, no. 2 (2009): 172–88, doi:10.1177/1069072708328897.

23. Jennifer Sherman and Rayna Sage, "Sending Off All Your Good Treasures: Rural Schools, Brain-Drain, and Community Survival in the Wake of Economic Collapse," *Journal of Research in Rural Education* 26, no. 11 (2011): 1–14.

24. Aaron Gettinger, "One Reason Rural Students Don't Go to College: Colleges Don't Go to Them," NPR.org, March 6, 2019, https://www.npr.org/2019/03/06/697098684/one-reason-rural-students-dont-go-to-college-colleges-don-t-go-to-them.

25. D. M. Dees, "'How Do I Deal with These New Ideas?': The Psychological Acculturation of Rural Students," *Journal of Research in Rural Education* 21 (2006), http://www.umaine.edu/jrre/21-6.pdf.

26. Aaron Gettinger, "A Big Reason Rural Students Never Go to College: Colleges Don't Recruit Them," *Hechinger Report*, March 6, 2019, https://hechingerreport.org/a-big-reason-rural-students-never-go-to-college-colleges-dont-recruit-them.

27. Victoria Rosenboom and Kristin Blagg, "Disconnected from Higher Education: How Geography and Internet Speed Limit Access to Higher Education," Urban Institute, January 2018, https://www.urban.org/sites/default/files/publication/96191/disconnected_from_higher_education_2.pdf.

28. Rosenboom and Blagg.

29. Rosenboom and Blagg.

30. Paul Fain, "Race, Geography and Degree Attainment," Inside Higher Ed, June 27, 2019, https://www.insidehighered.com/news/2019/06/27/rural-areas-lag-degree-attainment-while-urban-areas-feature-big-racial-gaps.

31. Rosenboom and Blagg, "Disconnected from Higher Education."

32. Colleen Campbell, "Those Left Behind," Center for American Progress, June 27, 2019, https://www.americanprogress.org/issues/education-postsecondary/reports/2019/06/27/471242/those-left-behind.

33. Geoff Marietta, Sky Marietta, Ada Smith, and Eagle Brosi, The Intersection of Education, Leadership, and High-Tech Industry in Rural Low-Income Communities (Chicago: American Educational Research Association Conference, 2015).

34. National Center for Education Statistics, "Dual Enrollment: Participation and Characteristics," NCES 2019-176, February 2019, https://nces.ed.gov/pubs2019/2019176.pdf.

35. Kevin Richert, "As Dual Credit Grows, Will Rural Students Get Left Behind?," Idaho Education News, May 30, 2018, https://www.idahoednews.org/news/as-dual-credit-grows-will-rural-students-get-left-behind.

36. Richert.

37. Richert.

38. Jessica Poiner, "In Ohio's Rural Districts, Innovation Is the Name of the Game," Thomas B. Fordham Institute, February 13, 2019, http://fordham institute.org/ohio/commentary/ohios-rural-districts-innovation-name-game.

39. Amadou Diallo, "Rural Schools Join Forces to Make College the Rule Rather than the Exception," Hechinger Report, November 16, 2017, https://hechinger report.org/rural-schools-join-forces-make-college-rule-rather-exception.

40. Diallo.

41. Diallo.

42. Diallo.6/29/20 7:18:00 PM

43. Battelle for Kids, "Rural Education Collaboratives: A Closer Look," 2016, https://battelleforkids.org/docs/default-source/publications/rec-case-studyoacfinal.pdf?sfvrsn=2.

44. Jeremy House, "Qualified Dual-Credit Teachers Hard to Recruit, Keep in Rural Areas," Education Dive, January 24, 2018, https://www.educationdive.com/news/qualified-dual-credit-teachers-hard-to-recruit-keep-in-rural-areas/515430.

45. House.

46. "Perkins V," Perkins Collaborative Resource Network, https://cte.ed.gov/legislation/perkins-v.

47. "Perkins V."

48. Dan Restuccia, Bledi Taska, and Scott Bittle, "Different Skills, Different Gaps: Measuring & Closing the Skills Gap," Burning Glass Technologies, March 2018, https://www.uschamberfoundation.org/sites/default/files/Skills_Gap_Different_Skills_Different_Gaps_FINAL.pdf.

49. "Apprenticeship," US Department of Labor, https://www.doleta.gov/oa/data_statistics2018.cfm.

50. "Career Development Incentive Program: Fact Sheet," Colorado Department of Education, https://www.cde.state.co.us/communications/oprfactsheet-career-development-incentive-prog.

51. "Career Development Incentive Program."

52. CareerWise Colorado, "CareerWise Launches Second Cohort with 126 Modern Youth Apprentices," July 3, 2018, https://www.careerwisecolorado.org/wp-content/uploads/2018/12/NR_CareerWise_2018kickoff_vfff-2.pdf.

53. "About P-TECH," P-TECH, http://www.ptech.org/about.

54. "Our Schools," P-TECH, http://www.ptech.org/p-tech-network/our-schools/usa.

55. Laura Pappano, "Colleges Discover the Rural Student," *New York Times*, January 31, 2017, sec. Education, https://www.nytimes.com/2017/01/31/education/edlife/colleges-discover-rural-student.html; Margaret Spellings, "UNC's Plan Seeks to Close the Gap Between the 'Two North Carolinas,'" *News & Observer*, December 16, 2017, https://www.newsobserver.com/opinion/op-ed/article 190172169.html; Eric Stirgus, "UGA President Announces Plans to Help Rural and Low-Income Students," *Atlanta Journal-Constitution*, January 24, 2018, https://www.ajc.com/news/local-education/uga-president-announces-plans-help-rural-and-low-income-students/ypTcilTRMyTKbRTOh2iIEO/; EAB, "Why Colleges Are Working to Win Over Skeptical Rural Students," December 7, 2017, https://www.eab.com/daily-briefing/2017/12/07/how-and-why-colleges-are-recruiting-rural-students.

56. Niswonger Foundation, http://www.niswongerfoundation.org.

57. "Maine Track MD," Tufts University School of Medicine, https://medicine.tufts.edu/education/MD-maine-track.

58. Gallup, *Alumni of Tribal Colleges and Universities Better Their Communities*, 2019, https://collegefund.org/wp-content/uploads/2019/12/Gallup_Report_Final_8-1-19.pdf.

59. D. Michael Pavel, Ella Inglebret , and Susan Rae Banks, "Tribal Colleges and Universities in an Era of Dynamic Development," *Peabody Journal of Education* 76, no. 1 (2001): 50–72, doi:10.1207/S15327930PJE7601_04.

Chapter 8

1. Louise Stoll et al., "Professional Learning Communities: A Review of the Literature," *Journal of Educational Change* 7, no. 4 (2006): 221–58, doi:10.1007/s10833-006-0001-8.

2. Miriam Jorgensen, *Rebuilding Native Nations: Strategies for Governance and Development* (Tucson: University of Arizona Press, 2007).

3. Eliot Wigginton, *Sometimes a Shining Moment: The Foxfire Experience* (Garden City, NY: Anchor Books, 1986); Shirley Brice Heath, *Ways with Words: Language, Life, and Work in Communities and Classrooms* (Cambridge, England: Cambridge University Press, 1983); Sylvia Ashton-Warner, *Spearpoint: Teacher in America* (New York: Knopf, 1972).

4. The National Education Association has a toolkit devoted to building cultural competence for educators: "Diversity Toolkit: Cultural Competence for Educators," NEA, http://www.nea.org/tools/30402.htm.

5. John Haaga, "Educational Attainment in Appalachia," Appalachian Regional Commission, July 2004, https://www.arc.gov/research/researchreportdetails .asp?REPORT_ID=35.

6. Lynne Vernon-Feagans and Martha Cox, "The Family Life Project: An Epidemiological and Developmental Study of Young Children Living in Poor Rural Communities," *Monographs of the Society for Research in Child Development* 78, no. 5 (2013): 1–126, doi:10.1111/mono.12047.

7. Kai A. Schafft, "Rural Education as Rural Development: Understanding the Rural School-Community Well-Being Linkage in a 21st-Century Policy Context," *Peabody Journal of Education* 91, no. 2 (2016): 137–54, doi:10.1080/01619 56X.2016.1151734.

8. Michael Lynch and Dante Cicchetti, "An Ecological-Transactional Analysis of Children and Contexts: The Longitudinal Interplay Among Child Maltreatment, Community Violence, and Children's Symptomatology," *Development and Psychopathology* 10, no. 2 (1998), 235–57.

9. Mara Casey Tieken, *Why Rural Schools Matter* (Chapel Hill: University of North Carolina Press, 2014).

10. Deborah Erwin, "An Ethnographic Description of Latino Immigration in Rural Arkansas: Intergroup Relations and Utilization of Healthcare Services," *Southern Rural Sociology* 19, no. 1 (2003): 46–72.

11. Harry M. Caudill, *Theirs Be the Power: The Moguls of Eastern Kentucky* (Urbana: University of Illinois Press, 1983); Elmore Leonard, *Fire in the Hole: Stories* (New York: Harper Collins, 2012).

12. Jorgensen, *Rebuilding Native Nations*.

13. Bruce Weber et al., "Upward Mobility of Low-Income Youth in Metropolitan, Micropolitan, and Rural America," *Annals of the American Academy of Political and Social Science* 672, no. 1 (2017): doi:10.1177/0002716217713477.

14. Cynthia M. Duncan, *World Apart: Why Poverty Persists in Rural America* (New Haven, CT: Yale University Press, 1999).

15. Peter Scales, Nancy Leffert, and Richard Lerner, *Developmental Assets: A Synthesis of the Research on Adolescent Development* (Minneapolis, MN: The Search Institute, 1999).

16. Tieken, *Why Rural Schools Matter*; Kai T. Erikson, *Everything in Its Path: Destruction of Community in the Buffalo Creek Flood* (New York: Simon & Schuster, 1978).

17. Stacey Childress and Geoff Marietta, *A Problem-Solving Approach to Designing and Implementing a Strategy to Improve Performance* (Cambridge, MA: Public Education Leadership Project, Harvard University, 2008), http://pelp.fas.harvard .edu/files/hbs-test/files/pel056p2.pdf.

18. Nonie Lesaux and Sky Marietta, *Making Assessment Matter: Using Test Results to Differentiate Instruction* (New York: Guilford Press, 2011).

19. AASA and the Rural School and Community Trust, *Leveling the Playing Field for*

Rural Students (Alexandria, VA: AASA, School Superintendents Association, November 2017), https://www.aasa.org/uploadedFiles/Policy_and_Advocacy/Resources/AASA_Rural_Equity_Report_FINAL.pdf.

20. Tieken, *Why Rural Schools Matter*.
21. Geoff Marietta, Chad D'Entremont, and Emily Murphy Kaur, *Improving Education Together: A Guide to Labor Management-Community-Collaboration* (Cambridge, MA: Harvard University Press, 2017).
22. "Alberta Family Wellness Initiative," Center of the Developing Child at Harvard University, https://developingchild.harvard.edu/collective-change/key-concepts/distributed-leadership/alberta-family-wellness-initiative.
23. Lesaux and Marietta, *Making Assessment Matter*.
24. Marietta, D'Entremont, and Kaur, *Improving Education Together*.

Chapter 9

1. US Department of Education, *Section 5005 Report on Rural Education* (Washington, DC: Department of Education, September 2018), https://www2.ed.gov/about/inits/ed/rural/rural-education-report.pdf.
2. Kai A. Schafft, "Rural Education as Rural Development: Understanding the Rural School-Community Well-Being Linkage in a 21st-Century Policy Context," *Peabody Journal of Education* 91, no. 2 (2016): 137–54, doi:10.1080/01619 56X.2016.1151734.
3. US Department of Education, *Section 5005 Report*.
4. Schafft, "Rural Education as Rural Development."
5. Stacey Childress and Geoff Marietta, "Invest Early: Early Childhood Development in a Rural Community" (HBS Case 309-089, Harvard Business School General Management Unit Research Paper, April 15, 2009).
6. Lisa Delpit and Joanne Kilgour Dowdy, eds., *The Skin That We Speak: Thoughts on Language and Culture in the Classroom* (New York: New Press, 2002); Patrick J. Finn, *Literacy with an Attitude: Educating Working-Class Children in Their Own Self-Interest*, 2nd ed. (Albany: SUNY Press, 2009); James Paul Gee, "Literacy, Discourse, and Linguistics: Introduction," *Journal of Education* 171, no. 1 (1989): 5–17, doi:10.1177/002205748917100101; Shirley Brice Heath, *Ways with Words: Language, Life, and Work in Communities and Classrooms* (Cambridge, England: Cambridge University Press, 1983); Peggy J. Miller, Grace E. Cho, and Jeana R. Bracey, "Working-Class Children's Experience Through the Prism of Personal Storytelling," *Human Development* 48, no. 3 (2005): 115–35, doi:10.1159/000085515.
7. "Relating to Rural Education; Declaring an Emergency," H.B. 4051, 79th Oregon Legislative Assembly, February 14, 2018, https://olis.leg.state.or.us/liz/2018R1/Downloads/MeasureDocument/HB4051/A-Engrossed.

8. "Infrastructure Grants: Overview," Wisconsin Technology for Educational Achievement, https://teach.wi.gov/Pages/Grants/InfrastructureGrants.aspx.

9. AASA and the Rural School and Community Trust, *Leveling the Playing Field for Rural Students* (Alexandria, VA: AASA: School Superintendents Association, November 2017), https://www.aasa.org/uploadedFiles/Policy_and_Advocacy/Resources/AASA_Rural_Equity_Report_FINAL.pdf.

10. Schafft, "Rural Education as Rural Development."

11. "By the Numbers," Apprenticeship Carolina, https://www.apprenticeship carolina.com/by-the-numbers.html.

12. Kristin Coulter, "Workforce Board Awards Workforce Innovation Grants," South Carolina Department of Employment and Workforce, August 12, 2018, http://palmettoconnections.dew.sc.gov/news-details-page/2018/08/16/workforce-board-awards-workforce-innovation-grants.

13. AASA and the Rural School and Community Trust, *Leveling the Playing Field*.

14. US Department of Education, *Section 5005*.

15. US Department of Education, *Section 5005*.

16. ARC, Power Virtual Workshop: RFP and Application Process, https://www.arc.gov/images/grantsandfunding/POWER2020/POWERVirtualWorkshopOverview.pdf.

17. "Where Americans Find Meaning in Life," Pew Research Center, November 20, 2018, https://www.pewforum.org/2018/11/20/where-americans-find-meaning-in-life.

ABOUT THE AUTHORS

GEOFF MARIETTA is entrepreneur-in-residence at the University of the Cumberlands and founder of Invest 606, a business accelerator and pitch contest for Southeastern Kentucky in partnership with the University of the Cumberlands, Foundation for Appalachian Kentucky, and the James Graham Brown Foundation. Geoff is also the founder of Mountain Tech Media, a diversified front-end digital media company based in Eastern Kentucky, and Trillium Ventures, a community development real estate company that invests and restores historic main street buildings in the region. He is the former executive director of Pine Mountain Settlement School, an eight-hundred-acre National Historic Landmark community nonprofit in Harlan County, Kentucky. Born in Hibbing, Minnesota, on the Mesabi Iron Range, Geoff attended the University of Montana, where he studied forestry. He then lived on the Navajo Nation in rural New Mexico, teaching high school special education and serving as an assistant principal. He went on to earn his MBA from Harvard Business School and a doctorate from the Harvard Graduate School of Education. During his time in Cambridge, Geoff cofounded and served as CEO of the software development company Giant Otter Technologies, acquired by Drift.com. In addition to *Rural Education in America*, Geoff is a coauthor of *Improving Education Together* and *Achieving Coherence in District Improvement*—as well as more than twenty case studies, articles, and reports. He currently lives in Williamsburg, Kentucky, with his wife, Sky, and their sons, Harlan and Perry.

––––––

SKY MARIETTA is an assistant professor at the University of the Cumberlands and director of the Learning Commons, a peer-based program to support the academic achievement of vulnerable college students. She also is the owner of Moonbow, a group of three small businesses that support Appalachian artists and suppliers on Main Street in Corbin, Harlan, and Williamsburg. Sky grew up in Appalachian Kentucky, the fifth of her parents' seven children. She went to college at Yale, became a teacher on the Navajo Nation, and then received her doctorate from the Harvard Graduate School of Education (HGSE) in child development with a focus on language and literacy. Rural communities have been a through line of her work, including a dissertation that examined the differences between early literacy development in urban and rural poor communities. She taught a class on rural education at HGSE as a post-doctoral fellow and lecturer. Since graduating, she has launched an early childhood program in Harlan County in Kentucky and worked as a specialist for Kentucky's Cooperative Extension program. In addition to *Rural Education in America*, she is a coauthor of *Teaching Advanced Literacy Skills* and *Making Assessment Matter*. She lives with her husband, Geoff, their sons, Harlan and Perry, and two dogs. She blogs about their lives and businesses at www.kentuckymoonbow.com.

INDEX

Addiction Recovery Care, 75
African American students and
    families
    high school graduation rates, 130–
        131
    increased integration benefitting,
        41–43
    internet access of, 114–115
    literacy and language development,
        96, 105–106
    percentage of population, 19
    rural economies relying on, 42
    teaching cultural history regarding,
        48–49
Alaska Native students and families
    access to childcare, 77
    views regarding outside agencies, 66
Alberta Family Wellness Initiative,
    165–166
All Children Are Equal Act (2012), 29
Appalachian Regional Commission,
    184
Apprenticeship Carolina, 183
Arizona, Rough Rock Demonstration
    School, 89
Arkansas
    access to medical care, 75–76
    integration in, 47
    outside perspective of, 34
    population instability in, 153–154

assessment and testing. see also self-
    improvement efforts for schools
    and districts
    cultural experience and knowledge
        affecting, 102–103
    by Early Learning Collaboratives, 83
    NAEP results, 47, 133
    participant action research as
        alternative to, 86
    PISA results, 112
    relevance and reliability of, in rural
        communities, 8, 55, 169, 184
asset map, 158–160

boomerang effect, 62–63

career and technical education (CTE),
    140–142
career opportunies. see college and
    career opportunities
cell phone service, 32–33
college and career opportunities. see
    also STEM education
    academic preparation of rural
        students for, 47, 133
    career and technical education
        (CTE) for, 140–142
    college efforts regarding, 135, 142–144

college and career opportunities,
    continued
  costs of, 134
  distance from colleges affecting, 48,
    135–136
  dual credit courses for, 138–140
  effects on wages, 131–132
  evaluation rubric for, 162
  golden cage experience in, 134
  mismatch with local opportunities,
    61–62, 64, 133–134, 136–138
  mismatch with rural culture, 135
  number of rural students interested
    in, 129, 132–133
  postsecondary educational
    attainment, 129–138
college and university partnerships,
    65, 119–120, 122, 126
Colorado, CTE in, 141–142
communities, rural. *see* rural
    communities
CTE (career and technical education),
    140–142
cultural context of rural communities.
    see social, cultural, and economic
    history

data walks, 155
demographics of rural communities,
    17–19, 27
digital divide, 32–33, 111, 113
disasters, community responses to,
    45–46
districts, rural. *see* rural schools and
    districts
diversity of rural communities
  increased integration benefitting,
    41–43
  local context of, including in
    education, 48–49
  statistics regarding, 18–19

dual credit courses, 138–140

early education and care
  adapting to community and family
    needs, 83–88
  childcare, 77–79
  economic vitality affecting, 72–74
  evaluation rubric for, 161
  goals of, 72, 87–88
  Head Start programs, 76, 77, 78, 83,
    87, 161
  importance of, 71, 76–77
  medical care, 75–76
  parent's addiction affecting, 74–75
  quality of, ensuring, 79–83
Early Learning Collaboratives, 82–83
economic history of rural
    communities. *see* social, cultural,
    and economic history
economic issues
  costs of childcare, 78–79
  costs of postsecondary education,
    131–132, 134
  effects on rural communities, 19–20,
    27–28
  family support with, 38
  local job opportunities affected by,
    61–62, 64, 133–134, 136–138
  upward mobility and, 38–39
economic vitality
  definition, 53–55
  educational achievement and, 72–76
  educational attainment and, 130, 134
  effects on rural education, 60–64
  self-assessment of, 152–153, 155, 156
ED (US Department of Education), 29
educational attainment
  high school graduation rates, 130–
    131, 133
  postsecondary educational
    attainment, 129–138

educational policies and improvement efforts. *see also* self-improvement efforts for schools and districts
  access and distribution of opportunities, 173, 183–184
  based on rural/urban designations, 23–24
  follow-through of, importance of, 179
  integrating with economic growth, 183
  local infrastructure, investment in, 181–182
  local leadership, investment in, 179, 180–181
  market-driven approaches, problems with, 8, 55, 169
  outside-led approaches, problems with, 170–178
  performance-based approaches, problems with, 8, 55, 169
  successful, guidelines for, 170, 180–186
  top-down approaches, problems with, 169–170, 178
education funding. *see* funding and grants
education in rural communities. *see* rural education; rural schools and districts
educators
  cultural knowledge of, 48–49
  qualifications and experience of, 46–48
  recruiting, challenges with, 48
  for STEM education, 115–116
Elementary and Secondary Education Act, 30
English language learners (ELLs), 91–92, 101
ethnic and racial diversity, 18–19, 41–43, 48–49

Family Life Project, 73–74, 78–79, 91, 94
family ties and social networks, 43–46, 158
Florida, Hillsborough County Public Schools, 20–21
food insecurity, 1, 29, 34, 47
foodways, connections to, 49–50
Frontier communities, 78
funding and grants
  based on rural/urban designations, 21, 24–25
  for career and technical education, 183–184
  collaborative arrangements for, 82–83, 182–183
  distributing across multiple organizations, 184
  from external agencies, 65–66, 170–178
  from foundations or philanthropists, 31, 80–81
  for health care, 22–23
  inequality of, 28–31
  for information technology infrastructure, 182
  integrating education with economic growth, 183
  from property taxes, 30–31
  from RECs, 120–122
  state and local formulas for, 30–31
  Title I and Title V funding, 29–30
  from university partnerships, 120

Georgia
  oral histories in, 89
  outside perspective of, 34
Giant Otter Technologies, 136–138
Golden Triangle Cooperative, 121
graduation rates. *see* educational attainment
grants. *see* funding and grants

Head Start programs, 76, 77, 78, 83, 87, 161

health care. *see also* food insecurity
access to, 74–76
careers in, 111–112
government funding for, 22–23
health outcomes in rural communities, 33–34
medical school scholarships and, 143
opiod epidemic, 74–75
parity of services, 41
partnerships with providers, 75–76
schools as delivery mechanism for, 34, 44

HHS (US Department of Health and Human Services), 22–23

Hispanic/Latino students and families. *see also* immigrant and migrant populations
access to childcare, 77
access to medical care, 76
high school graduation rates, 130–131
increased integration benefitting, 41–42, 47
internet access of, 114–115
percentage of population, 18–19

historical context of rural communities. *see* social, cultural, and economic history

Home-School Study of Language and Literacy Development (HSSLD), 94

Idaho
CTE (career and technical education) in, 142
dual credit courses in, 139
Khan Academy in, 118

IES (Institute of Education Sciences), 23–24

Illinois, STEM education in, 119

Imagination Library, 99–100

immigrant and migrant populations
access to medical care, 76
increased integration benefitting, 47
irregular work hours affecting, 74
literacy and language development for, 95
population instability from, effects on schools, 56–59, 153–154
rural economies relying on, 41–42

improvement efforts
inside efforts. *see* self-improvement efforts for schools and districts
outside efforts. *see* educational policies and improvement efforts

income and wages. *see also* economic vitality
postsecondary attainment affecting, 131–132
trends in, 134

Indiana, FFA in, 125–126

infrastructure of rural communities, 31–33

infrastructure of rural schools and districts, 181–182

in-migration. *see* immigrant and migrant populations

Institute of Education Sciences (IES), 23–24

internet access
affecting access to STEM education, 113–115
digital divide regarding, 32–33, 111, 113
improvement efforts including, 181–182

Invest Early, 81–82, 83, 87, 181

Iowa, population instability in, 7, 54, 56–58

Johnson, Lyndon B., 76

Kahn Academy, 182
Kentucky
    Addiction Recovery Care, 75
    bell hooks' experiences in, 42–43
    cell phone service, 32
    church membership, 107
    distance to library, 99
    diversity in, 42
    foundation funding, 31
    Giant Otter Technologies, 136–138
    Imagination Library, 99–100
    Kentucky Valley Education
        Cooperative (KVEC), 121, 181
    literacy and language development, 91
    Little School, 83–87, 175
    opiod epidemic, 12, 34
    oral histories in, 106
    outside perspective of, 34
    Pine Mountain Settlement School,
        4–5
    postsecondary educational
        attainment, 64
    President Johnson in, 76
    quality of education in, 46–47
    residential public high schools, 123
    transportation infrastructure, 32
    unemployment rate, 60
    University of Cumberlands (UC),
        143–144
    Williamsburg Independent School,
        1–2
KVEC (Kentucky Valley Education
    Cooperative), 121, 181

Latino students and families. see
    Hispanic/Latino students and
    families
learning communities
    focusing on school improvement.
        see professional learning
        communities (PLCs)
    focusing on STEM education, 119
Leveling the Playing Field for Rural
    Students, 182–183
literacy and language development
    academic language skills, 100–101,
        104, 108–109
    access to printed material, 98–100
    for ELLs, 91–92, 101
    evaluation rubric for, 161
    language skills, 91–97
    phonics skills, 90–91
    relevance to place, 89–90
    vocabulary development, 93–96, 98,
        102–104, 108–109
Little School, 83–87, 175
Louisiana, outside perspective of, 34

Maine, medical school scholarships
    in, 143
medical care. see health care
Microsoft's TEAL program, 182
migration in and out of rural
    communities. see immigrant and
    migrant populations; out-
    migration
Minnesota
    boomerang effect, 63
    early education and care, 80–81, 181
minorities. see specific groups
Mississippi
    government funding for, 29
    outside perspective of, 34
Mississippi First, 82, 83, 87
mobility. see relocation; upward mobility
Montana
    Golden Triangle Cooperative, 121
    Montana Artrepreneur Program, 142

National Center for Education
    Statistics (NCES), 23

National Institute for Early Education
    Research (NIEER), 83
Native American students and
    families
    access to childcare, 77
    community history regarding, 66–67
    cultural experience and knowledge
        of, 102–103
    oral histories of, 150–151
    percentage of population, 19
    Rough Rock Demonstration School
        and, 49, 89
    stereotypes regarding, 95
    teaching cultural history regarding,
        49
    Tribal Colleges and Universities
        (TCUs) and, 143
    views regarding outside agencies, 66
natural world, connections to, 49–50
NCES (National Center for Education
    Statistics), 23
New Mexico
    Navajo Nation schools in, 2–3, 102
    oral histories in, 150
NIEER (National Institute for Early
    Education Research), 83
North Carolina
    Family Life Project in, 73, 91
    residential public high schools in,
        122–123
North Dakota
    population instability in, 59, 63
    STEM education in, 119

Office of Management and Budget
    (OMB), 22
Ohio
    dual credit courses in, 139–140
    STEM education in, 112, 119, 121
OMB (Office of Management and
    Budget), 22

online and remote courses, 117–118. see
    also internet access
opiod epidemic, 33–34
Oregon
    childcare shortages in, 77
    Oregon's House Bill 4051, 181
out-migration
    effects on rural communities, 28,
        30–31
    reasons for, 61–62

participant action research, 86
partnerships. see also professional
        learning communities (PLCs)
    college and university partnerships,
        65, 119–120, 122, 126, 162
    community leadership affecting, 55,
        64–65
    with community organizations, 158,
        162
    for CTE apprenticeships, 141, 183
    including early childhood
        providers, 88
    with medical care providers, 75–76
    with outside-led improvement
        approaches, 170–178
    for STEM education, 117–123, 125–
        126, 136–138
Partnerships for Opportunity and
    Workforce and Economic
    Revitalization (POWER), 183
PELP Problem-Solving Framework,
    160–163
Pennsylvania
    Family Life Project in, 73, 91
    government funding for, 29
    STEM education in, 119
Pine Mountain Settlement School,
    4–5
PLCs. see professional learning
    communities (PLCs)

PLTW (Project Lead the Way), 118–119,
    182
policies and practices. *see* educational
    policies and improvement efforts
population of rural communities
    stability of, affecting education, 56–
        59, 153–154
    statistics regarding, 17–18, 27
postsecondary educational attainment,
    129–138. *see also* college and career
    opportunities
poverty. *see also* economic vitality;
        income and wages
    academic assessments and, 47
    child education and care supports,
        81–82
    educational resources lacking for, 3
    food insecurity and, 1, 29, 34, 47
    literacy and, 93, 98
    rates of, 12, 28
    self-assessment of, 153, 156
    Title I funding and, 29
    War on Poverty, 76
POWER (Partnerships for
    Opportunity and Workforce and
    Economic Revitalization), 183
professional learning communities (PLCs)
    asset map created by, 158–160
    data walks by, 155
    definition, 148
    leading school improvement efforts,
        160–167
    rubric used by, 160–162
    self-assessment by, 148–162
    timeline created by, 151–152
Project Lead the Way (PLTW), 118–119,
    182
property taxes, 30–31

racial and ethnic diversity, 18–19, 41–
    43, 48–49

racial and socioeconomic integration,
    39, 40–43, 157
racism, 42–43
RECs (rural educational cooperatives),
    120–122
relocation
    returning to rural communities, 37,
        62–63, 134, 137–138, 143
    to rural communities. *see* immigrant
        and migrant populations
    from rural communities. *see* out-
        migration
    statistics regarding, 37–38
Rennie Center for Education Research
    and Policy, 165
residential public high schools, 122–
    123
RLIS (Rural and Low-Income School
    Program), 29–30
Rough Rock Demonstration School, 89
RUCA (Rural-Urban Commuting
    Areas), 23
Rural and Low-Income School
    Program (RLIS), 29–30
rural communities
    definitions of, based on lived
        experience, 24–27
    definitions of, by federal agencies,
        20–24, 25
    demographics of, 17–19, 27
    economy's effects on, 19–20, 27–28
    family ties and social networks in,
        43–46, 158
    funding for, based on federal
        designation, 21, 24
    funding for, inequality of, 28–31
    health outcomes in, 33–34
    historical context of, social and
        economic. *see* social, cultural, and
        economic history
    infrastructure of, problems with,
        31–33

rural communities, continued
  inside perspective of, 35–36, 39–51
  leadership of, affecting education,
    55, 64–66, 154–155
  leadership of, investment in, 179,
    180–181
  natural world, connections to, 49–50
  outside perspective of, 17–18, 19–20,
    34–35, 37
  population of, 17–18, 27, 56–59, 153–154
  racial and ethnic diversity of, 18–19,
    41–43, 48–49
  reasons people stay in or return to,
    37–39, 61–62, 134, 137–138, 143
  socioeconomic and racial
    integration of, 39, 40–43, 157
  stereotypes regarding, 94–95
  strengths of, 39–50, 155–160
  variations across, 7, 35, 48–49, 53, 55
rural education
  college and career opportunities. see
    college and career opportunities
  community leadership affecting, 55,
    64–66, 154–155
  early childhood education. see early
    education and care
  economic vitality affecting. see
    economic vitality
  education policies affecting. see
    educational policies and
    improvement efforts
  forces affecting, 53–56, 66–68
  funding for. see funding and grants
  literacy and language development.
    see literacy and language
    development
  performance measurements,
    challenges with, 8, 55, 169, 184
  quality of, 46–49
  self-assessment and improvement
    of. see self-improvement efforts
    for schools and districts

  STEM education. see STEM
    education
  strengths of, 46–49, 156–158
rural educational cooperatives (RECs),
    120–122
rural schools and districts
  leading improvement efforts of,
    160–167
  outside improvement efforts for. see
    educational policies and
    improvement efforts
  residential public high schools, 122–
    123
  self-assessment of, 148–162
  social services and support provided
    by, 44–46
  standalone STEM schools, 123
Rural-Urban Commuting Areas
  (RUCA), 23

Save the Children, 171
schools, rural. see rural education;
    rural schools and districts
School Superintendent Association, 34
science, technology, engineering, and
    math (STEM) education. see STEM
    education
science, technology, engineering, arts,
    and math (STEAM) education,
    111–112, 113
self-improvement efforts for schools
    and districts
  leading improvement efforts, 160–167
  self-assessment for, 148–162
Small, Rural School Achievement
    Program (SRSA), 29–30
social, cultural, and economic history
  learning about, 149–152
  natural world included in, 49–50
  postsecondary graduation affected
    by, 130–138

rural education affected by, 8–9, 53–
   56, 66–68
self-assessment of, 149–152
social networks and family ties, 43–
   46, 158
socioeconomic and racial integration,
   39, 40–43, 157
socioeconomic status
   internet access and, 114–115
   literacy and, 93
   mobility of, 38–39
South Carolina
   Apprenticeship Carolina, 183
   foundation funding, 31
   government funding for, 31
   residential public high schools in, 123
   Workforce Innovation and
      Opportunity Act, 183
South Dakota, rural and urban
   designations in, 22
SRSA (Small, Rural School
   Achievement Program), 29–30
STEAM (science, technology,
   engineering, arts, and math)
   education, 111–112, 113
STEM (science, technology,
   engineering, and math) education
   curriculum providers for, 118–119
   demand for, by students, 116–117
   development of, 111–113
   evaluation rubric for, 162
   internet access affecting, 113–115
   learning communities for, 119
   local standalone STEM schools for, 123
   online and remote courses for, 117–118
   place-based learning for, 124–126
   residential public high schools for,
      122–123
   role models and instructors for, 115–
      116
   rural educational cooperatives for,
      120–122

university partnerships for, 119–120,
   122, 126
Strengthening Career and Technical
   Education for the 21st Century
   Act, 184

teachers. see educators
TEAL program, 182
technology-based careers
   increase in, 111–112
   preparing students for. see STEM
      education
Tennessee
   Imagination Library, 99–100
   scholarship programs in, 143
   STEM education in, 120
testing. see assessment and testing
Title I funding, 29–30
Title V funding, 29–30
transportation infrastructure, 31–32
21st Century Community Learning
   Centers, 171

University of Cumberlands (UC), 143–
   144
university partnerships, 65, 119–120,
   122, 126
upward mobility, 38–39
urban communities
   agglomeration effects of, 19, 28,
      30
   definitions of, by federal agencies,
      21–23, 25
US Census Bureau
   definition of Frontier communities
      by, 78
   definitions of rural commuties by,
      21–23, 25, 27, 32
   number of people moving reported
      by, 37

US Department of Agriculture
    (USDA), 22–23
US Department of Education (ED), 29
US Department of Health and Human
    Services (HHS), 22–23
US Department of Veteran's Affairs
    (VA), 23

VA (US Department of Veteran's
    Affairs), 23

War on Poverty, 76
Washington, population instability in,
    95, 154
West Virginia
    disaster responses in, 45–46
    opiod epidemic, 12, 34
    STEM education in, 112, 119
Wisconsin, internet access in, 182
Workforce Innovation and
    Opportunity Act, 183